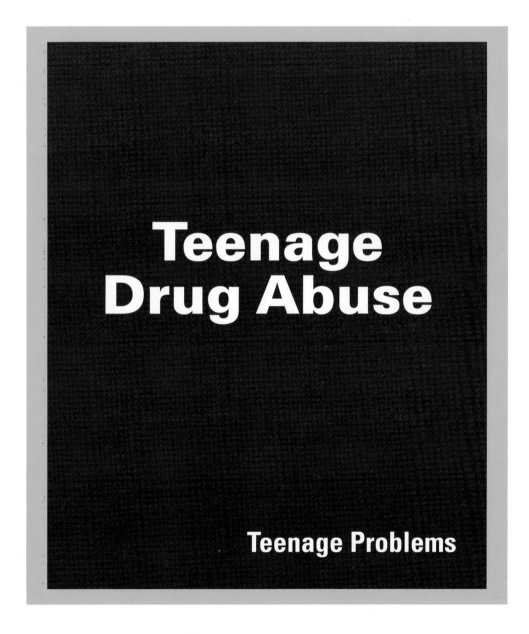

Teenage Drug Abuse

Teenage Problems

ReferencePoint
Press®

San Diego, CA

Other books in the Compact Research Teenage Problems set:

*For a complete list of titles please visit www.referencepointpress.com.

Teenage Drug Abuse

Leanne K. Currie-McGhee

Teenage Problems

ReferencePoint
Press®

San Diego, CA

For more information, contact:
ReferencePoint Press, Inc.
PO Box 27779
San Diego, CA 92198
www.ReferencePointPress.com

Picture credits:
Cover: iStockphoto.com and Thinkstock/Comstock
Maury Aaseng: 32–34, 46–49, 61–63, 75–77
Corbis/Ocean: 15
iStockphoto.com: 13

LIBRARY OF CONGRESS CATALOGING-IN-PUBLICATION DATA

Currie-McGhee, L. K. (Leanne K.)
   Teenage drug abuse / by Leanne Currie-Mcghee.
     p. cm. — (Compact research)
   Includes bibliographical references and index.
   ISBN-13: 978-1-60152-165-1 (hardback)
   ISBN-10: 1-60152-165-0 (hardback)
   1. Teenagers—Drug use—United States—Juvenile literature. 2. Drug abuse—Treatment—United States—Juvenile literature. 3. Teenagers—Drug use—United States—Prevention—Juvenile literature. I. Title.
   HV5824.Y68C87   2012
   618.92'86—dc22

                                              2010046672

Contents

Foreword

As modern civilization continues to evolve, its ability to create, store, distribute, and access information expands exponentially. The explosion of information from all media continues to increase at a phenomenal rate. By 2020 some experts predict the worldwide information base will double every 73 days. While access to diverse sources of information and perspectives is paramount to any democratic society, information alone cannot help people gain knowledge and understanding. Information must be organized and presented clearly and succinctly in order to be understood. The challenge in the digital age becomes not the creation of information, but how best to sort, organize, enhance, and present information.

ReferencePoint Press developed the *Compact Research* series with this challenge of the information age in mind. More than any other subject area today, researching current issues can yield vast, diverse, and unqualified information that can be intimidating and overwhelming for even the most advanced and motivated researcher. The *Compact Research* series offers a compact, relevant, intelligent, and conveniently organized collection of information covering a variety of current topics ranging from illegal immigration and deforestation to diseases such as anorexia and meningitis.

The series focuses on three types of information: objective single-author narratives, opinion-based primary source quotations, and facts and statistics. The clearly written objective narratives provide context and reliable background information. Primary source quotes are carefully selected and cited, exposing the reader to differing points of view. And facts and statistics sections aid the reader in evaluating perspectives. Presenting these key types of information creates a richer, more balanced learning experience.

For better understanding and convenience, the series enhances information by organizing it into narrower topics and adding design features that make it easy for a reader to identify desired content. For example, in *Compact Research: Illegal Immigration*, a chapter covering the economic impact of illegal immigration has an objective narrative explaining the various ways the economy is impacted, a balanced section of numerous primary source quotes on the topic, followed by facts and full-color illustrations to encourage evaluation of contrasting perspectives.

The ancient Roman philosopher Lucius Annaeus Seneca wrote, "It is quality rather than quantity that matters." More than just a collection of content, the *Compact Research* series is simply committed to creating, finding, organizing, and presenting the most relevant and appropriate amount of information on a current topic in a user-friendly style that invites, intrigues, and fosters understanding.

Teenage Drug Abuse at a Glance

Drug Abuse Among Teens

The *2009 National Survey on Drug Use and Health* found that an estimated 22.5 million persons in the United States were suffering from substance addiction or abuse; of these, 1.8 million were 12 to 17 years old.

Most Common Drugs

The most common substances abused by US teenagers are alcohol and
marijuana. Prescription drugs are the third most abused substance among
tenth and twelfth graders.

Internet Impact

The Internet has made it easier for teenagers to obtain, without a prescription, prescription drugs such as Vicodin and oxycodone.

Risky Behavior

When teenagers use drugs or alcohol they are more likely to indulge in
risky behavior such as unprotected sex, driving while high or drunk, and
getting into fights.

Damage to the Developing Brain

A teenager's brain is not fully developed and can be damaged by excessive
use of drugs or alcohol. The prefrontal cortex, which allows people to
understand situations and make sound decisions while keeping emotions
and desires under control, is especially susceptible to harm.

Addiction Risk

Teenagers who try alcohol or drugs are more likely than teenagers who never use these substances to become addicts as they get older.

Health Hazards

Drug and alcohol abuse can lead to physical problems including liver disease, lung cancer, and stroke—all of which can be fatal.

Getting Off Drugs

Teenage drug users most often turn to self-help groups for assistance in overcoming addiction. Residential and off-site treatment centers and counseling have also proved useful for beating teen drug and alcohol addiction.

How Medications Help

Various medications can help teen addicts fight cravings and withdrawal symptoms resulting from addiction to tobacco, drugs, and alcohol.

Overview

"Adolescents warrant increased attention because they are at heightened risk for drug abuse, they may suffer more severe consequences, and childhood and early adolescence represent times when targeted prevention efforts may have the most impact."

—Nora Volkow, director of the National Institute on Drug Abuse.

"When it comes to teen substance abuse, it seems like we're always playing catch up. Anytime a new drug hits the streets, its popularity soars, and we find ourselves fighting against it. At the same time, drugs that have been around for years sometimes rise sharply and unexpectedly in popularity."

—ASK (Adolescent Substance Abuse Knowledge Base), an educational website.

How Serious Is Teenage Drug Abuse?

Millions of young people in the United States endanger themselves and others by abusing drugs, alcohol, and tobacco every year. Each year the US Substance Abuse and Mental Health Services Administration (SAMHSA) conducts a nationwide survey on drug and alcohol use. According to the agency's *2009 National Survey on Drug Use and Health*, approximately 5.4 percent of young people in the United States between the ages of 12 and 20 (2.1 million) reported that they were heavy alcohol drinkers. In the same survey, 10 percent of youths aged 12 to 17 (2.5 million) reported that they were illicit drug users.

Additionally, 11.6 percent of 12- to 17-year-olds (2.9 million) reported that they used tobacco products.

Over the years, teenage use of certain types of drugs has decreased while use of other types has increased. According to the National Institute of Drug Abuse's 2009 *Monitoring the Future: National Results on Adolescent Drug Use* survey, an annual survey of attitudes and values of American secondary school students, the drug most often abused by teens in eighth, tenth, and twelfth grades is alcohol, followed by marijuana. Over the past decade, prescription drug abuse has also become popular. According to a 2010 survey conducted by the US Centers for Disease Control and Prevention, one in five high school students in the United States has taken a prescription medication that was not prescribed for them. Additionally, the 2009 *Monitoring the Future* survey reported that for tenth and twelfth graders, the third most abused drug, following alcohol and marijuana, was Vicodin (a prescription medication for pain). No matter what drugs teens abuse, the result is that these teenagers put themselves at risk for driving while impaired, getting into fights, engaging in risky sex, getting poor grades, and developing physical and emotional problems.

> " **Studies show that people are trying drugs at younger ages.** "

How Drugs Affect the Body

When people use drugs or alcohol, the substance alters the way their brains and bodies function. Alcohol, for instance, is a depressant that temporarily slows down the central nervous system, which consists of the brain and spinal cord. Additionally, alcohol blocks out some of the messages that try to get through to the brain. As a result, when people drink alcohol they initially become more relaxed and less inhibited; as they drink more, their vision becomes blurred, they slur their speech, their body movements become uncoordinated, and their judgment becomes impaired. Because their bodies are mature, adults who drink the same amount as teens typically do not feel the effects as quickly or intensely as teens. Many teens are still growing and have not achieved full height and weight, so even a small amount of alcohol can cause them to feel its effects.

Another popular teenage substance, marijuana, also alters a person's brain and body functions. When smoked, the chemical component tetrahydrocannabinol (THC) in marijuana rapidly passes from the lungs into the bloodstream, which then carries the THC to the brain and other organs throughout the body. The THC acts upon specific sites in the brain, causing users to experience the sensation of being "high." During this "high," a person is also affected by distorted perceptions, impaired coordination, and difficulty in thinking and problem solving. As with alcohol, because adolescents generally have smaller body sizes than adults and a lower tolerance for substances, these effects are more immediate.

> " **Prescription painkillers are frequently found in home medicine cabinets.** "

When used for nonmedical purposes, prescription drugs have serious effects on teen users as well. The most commonly abused prescription drugs are the opioids oxycodone (Oxycontin), hydrocodone (Vicodin), and meperidine (Demerol), all of which are typically prescribed for pain relief. Opioids attach to receptors in the central nervous system and prevent the brain from receiving pain messages. Opioids produce a quick, intense feeling of pleasure that is followed by a sense of well-being and a calm drowsiness. A person's ability to react quickly to situations is impaired by this type of drug. Opioids, like all drugs and alcohol, cause teenagers to not be fully in control of their physical and mental actions.

Younger First-Time Users

Studies show that people are trying drugs at younger ages, which increases their chances of becoming long-term substance abusers. According to the *2009 National Survey on Drug Use and Health*, in that year the average age of those who first tried illicit drugs was 17.6 years, which was significantly lower than the 2008 estimate of 18.8 years.

Health professionals warn that the younger people are when they try drugs or alcohol, the higher their risk for becoming addicted to those substances. Michael Dennis, senior research psychologist at Chestnut Health Systems in Bloomington, Illinois, reports that some 80 to 90 percent of people with substance abuse or dependence disorders started using under the age of 18, and half of these were under the age of 15. According to

Marijuana, one of the drugs most often abused by teenagers, can distort perception, impair coordination, and cause difficulty in thinking and problem solving. Some health experts believe it can also lead to experimentation with other drugs.

Ralph Hingston, director of the National Institute on Drug Abuse and Alcoholism epidemiology and prevention research division, "The younger people are when they first become intoxicated, the greater the likelihood that when they are in college they will meet alcohol-dependence criteria: that they will drive after drinking; that they will ride with drinking drivers; they will be injured under the influence of alcohol; or they will have unplanned and unprotected sex after drinking."[1]

Early Use Leads to Addiction

Megan Hakeman is an example of a teenager who started to use drugs at an early age and quickly found herself addicted. At age 13, Megan first tried marijuana when a neighbor offered it to her after learning that Megan felt depressed. Megan liked how the marijuana made her forget her problems and soon found herself using more and more drugs to cope with her life. She became addicted to huffing, which involves inhaling aerosol vapors to achieve a high. "Huffing was becoming a big problem, and an everyday occurrence. I did it alone, I did it with friends, I did it when I felt sad, lonely or scared—even when I was happy. It was my escape," writes Megan. "I did it anytime—I didn't care about family, friends, life or anything."[2]

At age 14 Megan entered treatment for drug addiction and, after much work, found new ways to cope with difficulties in life without using drugs. Like Megan, many young people who start using drugs or alcohol at an early age become dependent on those substances—and the consequences, in some cases, last a lifetime.

Easy Access

One of the factors that contributes to teen drug abuse is the relative ease with which teenagers can obtain drugs. Prescription painkillers such as Vicodin, for instance, are frequently found in home medicine cabinets. Teens also tell stories of using friends' prescription drugs such as Ritalin, which is frequently prescribed for attention deficit disorders. Teens sometimes share their drugs with each other or sneak a few samples from a friend's supply. About 64 percent of teens who have abused pain relievers say they got them from friends or relatives, often without their knowledge. Additionally, some teens are able to order prescription drugs online without a prescription, or they buy them from dealers who often order them online. "They're not very hard to get," says Paul Michaud, now 18, who first started taking Oxycontin pills as a freshman in high school and soon became addicted. "I could find [Oxycontin] easier than I could find pot. There were plenty of people who sold them."[3]

> " Many teenage drug abusers end up getting into trouble with the law. "

Huffing is also popular among youth because it is easy to obtain the products needed for huffing. People can huff from a wide variety of

Abuse of prescription drugs, which are often found in home medicine cabinets, is a growing problem among teenagers. After alcohol and marijuana, prescription drugs are the next most abused substance among tenth and twelfth grade students.

substances, including many common household products such as aerosol hairsprays or deodorants. Teenagers huff more than any other age group primarily because they can obtain these products with little trouble.

Substances such as alcohol and cigarettes are also relatively easy for teenagers to access since they can get older friends to purchase them legally. A 2010 survey of teens in Roanoke County, VA, found that 45 percent of middle school students and more than 80 percent of high school students said alcohol is "very easy" to obtain. Additionally in 2009, according to the *Monitoring the Future* survey, some 55 percent of eighth graders and 76 percent of tenth graders said that cigarettes would be easy to get. The ease of access of these substances leads to increased likelihood of using and subsequently abusing them.

What Are the Dangers of Teenage Drug Abuse?

Drug abuse can adversely affect all areas of a teenager's life—leading to physical, social, emotional, legal, and other problems. Substance abuse can lead to poor schoolwork, loss of friends, difficulties at home, and lasting legal problems. Additionally, at some point in their lives, many teenage drug abusers end up getting into trouble with the law.

Jason Solowes discovered this in June 2008 when he was arrested and charged with drug trafficking, manufacturing, and possession with intent to distribute. Solowes started using alcohol and marijuana as a young teenager and turned to methamphetamine by the time he was 15. He began to sell marijuana, pills, and cocaine to fund his own drug habit. Over the years, Solowes learned how to make methamphetamine—for sale and for his own use.

> " Teenagers are more susceptible to making poor decisions, such as giving in to peer pressure. "

After his arrest, Solowes spent two months in jail before he was given the opportunity to attend rehabilitation at the Herring Houses in Dolthan, AL. At the time, Solowes had no intention of quitting his drug use. "I didn't want to quit drinking and using, I just wanted to get out of trouble," Solowes said. "Going to rehab was just an avenue to get out of jail. I had been lying to myself for many years, I could've been so many things. I could've been a lawyer, a doctor, anything, but I chose to be a drug dealer, dope cook and a junkie."[4]

Solowes soon found that the long-term treatment program at Herring Houses could actually help him. He not only decided to get sober, he also chose to stay that way. Today Solowes is the patient administrator at the rehabilitation facility that gave him a second chance only a few years ago.

Teenagers More Prone to Addiction

Teenagers who experiment with drugs and alcohol are more susceptible than adults to developing an addiction. In both adults and teenagers, the brain releases chemicals such as dopamine during pleasurable activities such as drug use, and these chemicals make the person want to repeat the activities. A Yale University study found that during adolescence the brain releases an increased amount of chemicals such as dopamine whenever it undergoes a new experience. An adolescent feels the pull to try drugs again even more strongly than an adult because of the increased amounts of dopamine the adolescent's brain releases.

Another reason that young people are more susceptible to drug abuse and addiction than adults is that parts of the teenage brain that control reasoning are not fully developed. Frances Jensen, a pediatric neurologist at Children's Hospital in Boston, explains that the frontal lobes, crucial parts of the brain that process the consequences of one's actions, are not fully connected in teenagers. "It's the part of the brain that says: 'Is this a good idea? What is the consequence of this action?'" Jensen says. "It's not that they don't have a frontal lobe. And they can use it. But they're going to access it more slowly."[5] Because of this, teenagers are more susceptible to making poor decisions, such as giving in to peer pressure and trying drugs and alcohol, which then increases their chances of becoming abusers or addicts.

Binge Drinking a Problem

Binge drinking, the heavy consumption of alcohol over a short period of time, is increasing among teenagers and young adults. The National Institute on Alcohol Abuse and Alcoholism defines binge drinking as a pattern of drinking that brings a person's blood alcohol concentration (BAC) to 0.08 grams per deciliter of blood or above over a short period of time. This typically happens when men have five or more alcoholic drinks and when women consume four or more drinks in about two hours. According to the *2009 National Survey on Drug Use and Health*, in that year 8.8 percent of youth aged 12 to 17 reported that they had engaged in binge drinking.

Binge drinking can have serious consequences including death from alcohol poisoning and car accident deaths caused by intoxicated driving. From 2004 to 2007, doctors at the University of California's Davis Medical Center have seen a 30 percent increase in youth between 12 and 17 coming to the emergency room with trauma from binge drinking.

> **Thousands of young people in the United States seek treatment for drug and alcohol abuse each year.**

Leandra Ybarra suffered the consquences of binge drinking when she was just 15 years old. Leandra had skipped school with her friends to drink some rum. "I finished a whole bottle in less than 30 minutes or so. . . . The last thing I honestly remember is my fishing pole falling into the river, since we were down hill they had to actually drag me up,"[6] says Leandra. At the hospital, doctors discovered Leandra was near death from alcohol poisoning. She survived and now speaks to teenagers about the consequences of drinking.

How Is Teenage Drug Abuse Treated?

Thousands of young people in the United States seek treatment for drug and alcohol abuse each year. According to the *2009 National Survey on Drug Use and Health*, 1.8 million 12- to 17-year-olds were in need of substance abuse treatment. Teens have a variety of options for combating drug and alcohol addiction and finding other ways to deal with problems in their lives.

Of the 1.8 million American adolescents who needed treatment in 2009, 150,000 received treatment at specialty facilities, which include both residential and outpatient treatment centers. At a residential facility people must remain on site day and night, typically for 30 to 90 days; they go to counseling sessions, behavioral therapy, and group sessions to learn how to live their lives without depending on drugs or alcohol. At outpatient treatment facilities people come and go, attending counseling sessions and other types of therapy during the day and returning home at night.

Young people in the survey who did not get treatment at a center either did not get any treatment or received it in other ways. One way is for teenagers to attend personal counseling sessions and/or family counseling to help determine why they are turning to alcohol and drugs and to find healthier alternatives. Another option is to attend self-help groups such as Narcotics Anonymous or Alcoholics Anonymous where people meet with other substance abusers, are paired with a mentor who has maintained sobriety, and discuss ways they can cope with their everyday lives without getting high or drunk.

Centers Specializing in Teens and Young Adults

Experts say that on-site treatment centers designed specifically for teenagers are often the best option for combating abuse and addiction. These centers help teenagers figure out why they turn to drugs or alcohol and other ways to cope with their problems. Nearly 85 percent of young adults who undergo rehabilitation at treatment centers go to facilities that specialize in their age group.

In addition to the normal activities offered in adult drug treatment centers, such as group therapy and personal counseling, treatment centers for youth provide schooling so patients do not get behind in their education. Some also offer activities such as horseback riding or outdoor team games to help teenagers gain self-confidence and self-understanding and address issues that generally cause teens to turn to drugs and alcohol. Specifically, these centers focus on family problems, school issues, lack of confidence, and peer pressure—all of which are typical triggers of teenage alcohol and drug abuse.

> " **When parents talk regularly to their children about the dangers of drugs, they reduce the likelihood of their children using drugs.** "

Aspen Ranch in Loa, Utah, is a treatment center for 13- to 17-year-olds who are dealing with substance abuse, emotional issues, and/or grief issues. While at the center, teens attend group and individual therapy sessions in addition to school, which is individually paced. They also participate in the center's Equine Program in which they learn to ride, jump, and care for horses. Through team building, problem solving, and the like, the participants gain self-esteem and learn valuable life skills.

Can Teenage Drug Abuse Be Prevented?

Studies show that the longer young people can be prevented from trying drugs or alcohol, the less likely they are to one day develop a substance abuse problem. Teenagers can be discouraged in several ways from ever trying drugs and alcohol. One way is for parents to talk to their children honestly about drug use and its potential effects while their children are still young. According to the Partnership for a Drug-Free America, when parents talk regularly to their children about the dangers of drugs, they reduce the likelihood of their children using drugs by 42 percent compared with parents who do not talk to their children about this issue. However, despite the positive effects of being open and honest with teenagers about drugs, only a quarter of teenagers report that their parents have these types of conversations with them.

Schools and communities can also help prevent teens from using drugs by offering drug prevention programs that teach students the dangers of drugs and alcohol and what they can do to resist peer pressure. One example is D.A.R.E. (Drug Abuse Resistance Education), which is a nationwide program in which police officers come into schools to teach young people ways to avoid involvement in drugs, alcohol, tobacco use, gangs, and violence. Ultimately, D.A.R.E. is trying to achieve what all prevention programs aspire to—to delay or completely stop young people from experimenting with tobacco, drugs, or alcohol in order to reduce their chances of becoming abusers or addicts as they get older.

How Serious Is Teenage Drug Abuse?

> **66Adolescence is the time when most people become addicted.99**
>
> —Michael Dennis, senior research psychologist at Chestnut Health Systems in Bloomington, IL.

> **66After the death of my father in 2007, my sadness was so overwhelming I desperately was searching for something to take me out of myself so that I no longer had to feel. I started with alcohol and pot, only to quickly discover other drugs such as Roxicodone and Oxycontin. No person or any circumstance made me try drugs, I tried them out of curiosity and because I wanted to.99**
>
> —Sarah Alford, 20-year-old recovering addict.

Experimentation Leads to Abuse

D rug abuse is using drugs to the point at which the user's life is negatively impacted on a regular basis. Abuse is a problem for people of all ages, but it is particularly a problem for young people because it can seriously impact their lives for years to come. According to the *2009 National Survey on Drug Use and Health*, in that year an estimated 22.5 million persons in the United States were suffering from substance addiction or abuse. Of the 22.5 million who were dependent on drugs or alcohol, 1.8 million were 12 to 17 years old.

Millions of teens experiment with drugs and alcohol each year. In the United States an estimated 3.1 million persons aged 12 or older used an illicit drug for the first time during 2009—an average of 8,500 new users per day. About three-fifths of the new users were younger than age 18 when they first experimented.

> Drug abuse is using drugs to the point at which the user's life is negatively impacted on a regular basis.

Once of the reasons early experimentation with drugs and alcohol is a serious problem is that it heightens the risk of a person becoming dependent on alcohol or drugs as they get older. "Using alcohol and tobacco at a young age has negative health effects. While some teens will experiment and stop, or continue to use occasionally, without significant problems, others will develop a dependency, moving on to more dangerous drugs and causing significant harm to themselves and possibly others," states the American Academy of Child and Adolescent Psychiatry. "It is difficult to know which teens will experiment and stop and which will develop serious problems."[7]

Drugs Most Commonly Abused by Teenagers

The popularity of substances is tied to how easily a teen can obtain them. Although teens are not legally allowed to purchase alcohol, they can get it from older friends or siblings. According to an annual survey released by the Partnership for a Drug-Free America, 39 percent (6.5 million) of high school students in the United States said they drank alcohol in the month before the survey. Another popular substance among teens is cigarettes. According to the 2009 *Monitoring the Future* study, 1 out of 5 twelfth graders and 1 out of 15 eighth graders in the United States are smokers. Eighteen-year-olds can obtain cigarettes legally, so, as with alcohol, younger teens are able to get cigarettes from older friends or siblings.

The nonmedical use of prescription drugs such as pain relievers, tranquilizers, stimulants, and sedatives is also popular among teens because often they can get them from their home medicine cabinets, from friends, or by ordering online. Approximately one in five high school students in the United States admits to having taken a prescription drug without a doctor's prescription, the Centers for Disease Control and Prevention (CDC) says in its *2009 National Youth Risk Behavior Survey*.

Marijuana is another common drug used by teens. The Partnership for a Drug-Free America found that 6.7 percent of US youths aged 12 to 17 used the drug in 2009. Despite being illegal, teens report that marijuana is easy to obtain, which is why it has remained one of the most popular drugs used by teens for decades.

Why Teenagers Start Using Drugs

Every day, thousands of teenagers in the United States try drugs or alcohol for the first time. According to the Office of National Drug Control Policy, in the United States an estimated 1.64 million people aged 12 to 18 years used an illicit drug for the first time in 2008; this averages to 4,504 initiates per day. The reasons for trying drugs include, but are not limited to, peer pressure, emotional or family problems, being in surroundings where drugs are prevalent, having parents and/or other close family members who are substance abusers, and involvement in gangs.

One of the most common reasons teenagers first try drugs is that they find it relaxes them in social situations and helps them feel part of a group. For example, Nicole Hansen started to use drugs at age 17 to help her fit in at parties. "I decided to go to a party where I knew people would be doing drugs. Everyone seemed to know each other. I have to admit, I was jealous. I felt like an outsider," writes Hansen. "Halfway through the night I met a really awesome guy. After talking for a while he offered me Ecstasy. I decided to try it. As I swallowed the pill I thought, there's no way this could be bad. A half an hour went by and I began to question its power. But then it hit me like a tidal wave. It was incredible."[8] Hansen began taking Ecstasy on a regular basis, and her need for it grew to the point of addiction. One night Hansen overdosed and had stopped breathing before being revived by emergency room doctors. Since then,

> " **The nonmedical use of prescription drugs is also popular among teens.** "

she has remained drug free and takes part in drug prevention programs, speaking to audiences about her experiences.

Another common reason that teens use drugs is that they feel pressure to do so when in places where drugs are prevalent. One 2007 survey asked teens how common drug use was among the popular kids at their school. It also asked students to rate their school as being relatively drug-free or not drug-free. That survey, by the National Center on Addiction and Substance Abuse (CASA) at Columbia University, found that teens in schools where drug use was common were five and a half times more likely to identify the popular kids as being drug users and three times more likely to identify the popular kids as using alcohol. "This fall more than 16 million teens will return to middle and high schools where drug dealing, possession, use and students high on alcohol or drugs are part of the fabric of their school,"[9] said Joseph A. Califano Jr., CASA's chairman and president and former US secretary of health, education, and welfare, in 2007. He urged parents and others to work with schools to change this situation.

> **Children of alcoholics are four times more likely than other children to become alcoholics.**

Genetics Heightens Risk

Certain groups of teenagers are more likely than others to develop drug or alcohol problems. One group of teenagers at risk has close biological family members who are battling alcohol or drug abuse. Children of alcoholics are four times more likely than other children to become alcoholics, according to the American Academy of Child and Adolescent Psychiatry.

Although children of substance addicts are at higher risk for becoming addicts, that outcome is preventable. Evidence shows that while alcoholism is 50 to 60 percent determined by genetics, 40 to 50 percent is determined by environmental influences. A teen who knows about the high risk for alcoholism in his or her family can make use of this knowledge by avoiding alcohol. Additionally, the chance of becoming an addict can be decreased by getting involved in prevention programs that teach kids how to respond to peer pressure or by getting counseling to learn how to deal with problems without turning to drugs or alcohol.

Susceptible to Drug Abuse

In addition to genetics, other factors increase the risk of becoming a drug or alcohol abuser. One risk factor is growing up in places where drugs and alcohol are commonly used by close friends and family. Studies show that living in a home where drugs and alcohol are prevalent increases the risk of experimentation and abuse.

Teens who suffer from emotional or mental health problems are also at risk. According to the National Network for Childcare, more than 6 million young people in America suffer from a mental health disorder such as depression. Of these, approximately two-thirds do not get treatment. "Without treatment, a depressed teen may turn to alcohol or drugs to escape their feelings of helplessness or to help them feel 'normal,'"[10] states Casa Palmera, a treatment center for addiction.

> **Teenagers often start experimenting with 'gateway' drugs.**

Being at higher risk for drug abuse or addiction does not mean the teen is destined to become an addict. Instead, knowing that he or she is at risk can help such a teen to stand up to peer pressure and avoid experimenting. Also, if trusted adults understand the risks of teens they know, they can intervene by making the teens aware of substance abuse risks.

Gateway Drugs

Teenagers often start experimenting with "gateway drugs" such as marijuana, alcohol, and tobacco, which are considered less addictive and less physically harmful than harder drugs such as heroin, meth, and cocaine. The reason these substances are termed "gateway drugs" is that some people believe use of these drugs eventually leads to experimentation with and subsequent abuse of harder drugs.

The idea that these substances lead to the use of more dangerous drugs is supported by various studies and agencies. According to the *2010 CASA National Survey on American Attitudes on Substance Abuse*, teens who have tried tobacco are 12 times more likely to have used marijuana

than teens who have never tried tobacco. Additionally, the National Institute on Drug Abuse reports that long-term studies show that young
drug abusers often begin with marijuana and escalate from there. Others disagree that the use of substances such as
marijuana, alcohol, and tobacco leads to the
use of harder drugs. In December 2006 a 12-
year American Psychiatric Association study
of boys aged 10 to12 concluded that adolescents who used marijuana prior to using other
drugs, including alcohol and tobacco, were no
more likely to develop a substance abuse disorder than those who did not use marijuana
prior to using other drugs. Whether these
substances are gateway drugs or not continues to be debated, but, either
way, the drugs themselves can negatively impact teen users.

> " The Internet
> provides
> teenagers
> easy access
> to drugs. "

Impact of the Internet

The Internet is a portal to all kinds of information—some of it educational and helpful and some of it questionable and dangerous. Many
easily accessed websites provide Internet users with information about
getting high on substances ranging from aerosols to cough syrups.

The Internet also provides teenagers easy access to drugs. The Partnership for a Drug-Free America found that twelfth graders have been
able to purchase prescription drugs like Vicodin and Oxycontin online
without actually having a prescription. "Anyone of any age can obtain
dangerous and addictive prescription drugs with the click of a mouse,"
says Califano. "This problem is not going away."[11]

Multiple Addictions

Many people who abuse both drugs and alcohol use several different
types of drugs. Some drug abusers may use a stimulant like methamphetamine to get energy during the daytime, then turn to alcohol to settle
down at night. Others may abuse prescription drugs such as barbiturates
and benzodiazepines along with another substance or drug, such as alcohol or cocaine. The *2009 National Survey on Drug Use and Health* found
that 3.2 million people in the United States were considered dependent
on or abused both alcohol and illicit drugs.

Abuse of one substance is dangerous enough; mixing substances is even more dangerous. The National Institute on Drug Abuse reports that young people who abuse prescription drugs commonly mix them with other drugs, particularly alcohol, which amplifies the risk of overdose and even death. For example, a teenager may use a stimulant such as Ritalin without a prescription and then combine it with an over-the-counter drug such as cough syrup. From this, he or she can develop dangerously high blood pressure that can result in irregular heart rhythms, potentially resulting in death.

As millions of teens experiment with drugs and alcohol each year, the chance of many of them being harmed by combining substances is likely. But even if teens use only one substance, they are still putting their lives in danger. Substance abuse among teenagers is a serious problem that can lead to dangerous and at times fatal results.

How Serious Is Teenage Drug Abuse?

66 Using marijuana puts children and teens in contact with people who are users and sellers of other drugs. So there is more of a risk that a marijuana user will be exposed to and urged to try more drugs. 99

—National Institute on Drug Abuse (NIDA), "Marijuana: Facts for Teens," March 2008. www.nida.nih.gov.

NIDA is a US government institute with the mission to lead the country in using science to fight drug abuse and addiction.

66 Most marijuana users never use any other illegal drug. Indeed, for the large majority of people, marijuana is a terminus rather than a gateway drug. 99

—Drug Policy Alliance, "Marijuana," 2010. www.drugpolicy.org.

The Drug Policy Alliance is the nation's leading organization promoting policy alternatives concerning how the government legislates and regulates illegal drugs.

* Editor's Note: While the definition of a primary source can be narrowly or broadly defined, for the purposes of Compact Research, a primary source consists of: 1) results of original research presented by an organization or researcher; 2) eyewitness accounts of events, personal experience, or work experience; 3) first-person editorials offering pundits' opinions; 4) government officials presenting political plans and/or policies; 5) representatives of organizations presenting testimony or policy.

> **Adolescents who drink or use drugs before they turn 15 are more likely to fail in school, become dependent on drugs or alcohol, be convicted of a crime, contract a sexually transmitted disease, and face an unwanted pregnancy.**

—Adolescent Substance Abuse Knowledge (ASK) Base, "Preteen Drinking," June 2009. www.adolescent-substance-abuse.com.

ASK is a website sponsored by the CRC Health Group and provides people with information about teenage drug abuse.

> **Youth attitudes about the dangers of drugs have softened in the past couple of years. In the past this has often signaled that increases in use are coming.**

—Gil Kerlikowske, "White House Drug Policy Director Issues Statement on National Drug Survey," Office of National Drug Control Policy, September 16, 2010. www.whitehousedrugpolicy.gov.

Kerlikowske is the US Office of National Drug Control Policy director.

> **Teens are more likely to start experimenting with drinking if they have parents who drink, if they have friends who are also drinking, and if their parents don't give them clear messages about not drinking outside the house (if they are allowed to drink some wine with dinner, for instance).**

—Reid K. Hester, "Why Do Teenagers Drink Alcohol?" *Selfhelp Magazine*, August 18, 2008. www.selfhelpmagazine.com.

Hester is director of the research division at Behavior Therapy Associates.

> **I smoked my first joint with my mom. I was 10 years old. My mom said, 'You can drink and use, just as long as you're doing it with me.' I thought that was cool.**

—Chantel, "I Wanted the Life Other Girls Had," Check Yourself, 2009. http://checkyourself.com.

Chantel grew up surrounded by drugs and became an abuser herself. Today she is in recovery working to stay sober.

❝The Internet has become a key source of addictive, illicit drugs and a handy resource for other practices to sustain drug use.❞

—HBO, "Teens, the Internet and Illicit Drugs," 2010. www.hbo.com.

HBO produced the the Addiction Project in partnership with the Robert Wood Johnson Foundation, the National Institute on Drug Abuse (NIDA), and the National Institute on Alcohol Abuse and Alcoholism (NIAAA).

❝Alcohol? Cocaine? Hydrocodone? There are many drugs of choice, but no matter the substance, if you are addicted to one, you are addicted to it all.❞

—Sarah Senghas, "What Kind?" Associated Content, April 15, 2008. www.associatedcontent.com.

Senghas holds a master's degree in educational psychology and counselor education and writes health-related articles for various publications.

Facts and Illustrations

How Serious Is Teenage Drug Abuse?

- According to the *2009 National Survey on Drug Use and Health*, **7 percent** of youths aged 12 to 17 were classified as being dependent on drugs and/or alcohol.

- The illicit drug use rate increased from **9.3 percent** in 2008 to **10 percent** in 2009 among 12- to 17-year-olds, according to the *2009 National Survey on Drug Use and Health*.

- The 2009 *Monitoring the Future* survey reports that nearly three-quarters of students (**72 percent**) have consumed alcohol by the end of high school.

- The 2009 *Monitoring the Future* survey found that **47 percent** of students have used an illicit drug by the end of high school.

- The American Lung Association reports that every day in the United States almost **3,900** young people under 18 years of age try their first cigarette, and more than **950** of them will become regular daily smokers.

- According to a 2009 *Time*/Nickelodeon survey of young people aged 9 to 14, **36 percent** feel peer pressure to smoke marijuana, and **40 percent** feel pressure to drink.

- The American Lung Association has found that exposure to **pro-tobacco marketing and media** more than doubles the chances of children and adolescents starting tobacco use.

Teen Use of Alcohol, Marijuana, and Cigarettes

In 2009 the CDC surveyed a sample of high school students across the United States. This visual shows the percentage of students surveyed who admitted that they had drunk alcohol, used marijuana, or smoked cigarettes in the 30 days before the survey.

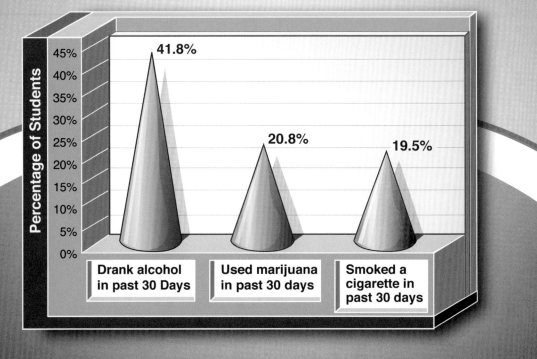

Source: Centers for Disease Control and Prevention, "2009 Youth Risk Behavior Survey Overview," 2009. www.cdc.gov.

- Based on the 2010 CASA National Survey on American Attitudes on Substance Abuse, compared with teens who say they are in drug- and gang-free schools, teens who attend schools with drugs and gangs are almost **12 times** more likely to have used tobacco and **five times** more likely to have used marijuana.

Prescription Drug Use Among High School Students, 2009

Nonmedical use of prescription drugs has become popular among high school students. In 2009 the CDC surveyed high school students. This chart shows what percentage of high school students, by grade, have taken prescription drugs without having a prescription.

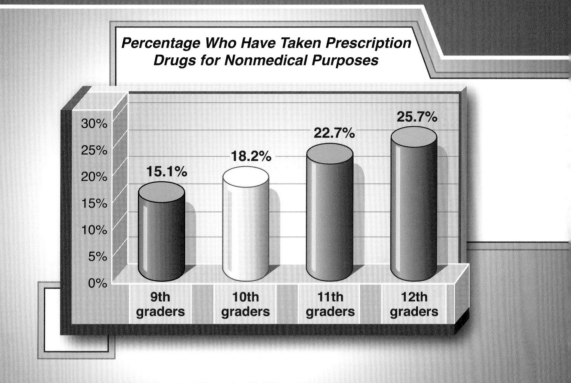

Percentage Who Have Taken Prescription Drugs for Nonmedical Purposes

- 9th graders: 15.1%
- 10th graders: 18.2%
- 11th graders: 22.7%
- 12th graders: 25.7%

Source: Centers for Disease Control and Prevention, *Morbidity and Mortality Weekly Report*, June 4, 2010. www.cdc.gov.

- The 2010 CASA National Survey on American Attitudes on Substance Abuse found that compared with teens who say none of their friends use marijuana, teens who report having any friends who use marijuana are **36 times** more likely to have tried marijuana themselves.

Trends in Teenage Illicit Drug Use, 1991–2009

Based on statistics from the *Monitoring the Future* studies, this chart shows what percentage of eighth, tenth, and twelfth graders in the United States have used drugs annually in the past 18 years. It shows a steep rise in the early 1990s, then a decline for several years, followed by a slow rise in the past few years.

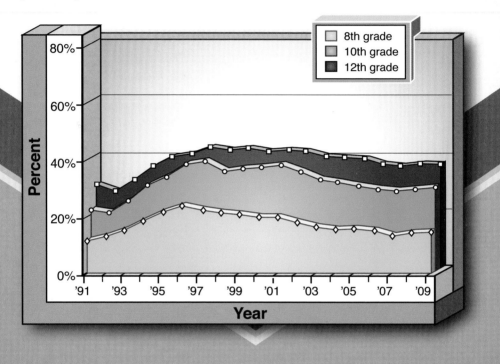

Source: *Monitoring the Future* survey, "Trends in Annual Prevalence of an Illicit Drug Use Index," 2009.
http://monitoringthefuture.org.

- The US Department of Health and Human Services found in 2009 that among adults who first tried alcohol at age 14 or younger, **17.5 percent** developed alcohol dependence or abuse compared with only **3.7 percent** of adults who had first used alcohol at age 18 or older.

What Are the Dangers of Teenage Drug Abuse?

66Drug use is associated with a variety of negative consequences, including increased risk of serious drug use later in life, school failure, and poor judgment which may put teens at risk for accidents, violence, unplanned and unsafe sex, and suicide.99

—American Academy of Child and Adolescent Psychiatry.

66It's important to note that adolescent high-risk behaviors cluster. Meaning, where there is drinking, it is safe to assume that there may be other drug use, sexual activity, and other risk-taking.99

—Jeff Wolfsburg, expert in drug education.

Risk of Addiction

One of the major dangers for teens who abuse drugs and alcohol is that excessive use increases their risk of addiction. Addiction is a craving so severe that satisfying it becomes the center of the addict's life. Even if the person's health, social life, education, or emotional well-being is suffering, he or she will continue to use the substance. Teenagers who experiment with drugs and alcohol increase their chances of becoming addicted in the future.

Addiction is the result of physical changes in the body. Certain drugs, such as methamphetamine or cocaine, change the way the brain communicates by disrupting the brain's neurotransmitters, which are what the brain uses to transmit information. When taking drugs, the brain's neurotransmitters tell the person to keep using the drugs in order to continue getting the pleasure or relief they give. The neurotransmitters can make this message so strong that the person feels that he or she cannot live without the drugs. A teenager feels this even more strongly than an adult because a teenage brain releases an increased amount of neurotransmitters such as dopamine whenever the teen has new experiences. A teen's brain will tell him or her to keep taking the drugs.

> A teen's brain will tell him or her to keep taking the drugs.

When teens become addicted to drugs or alcohol they endanger their physical and emotional health as well as relationships with friends and family. Getting and using drugs becomes the focus of their lives, and addiction can lead to dropping out of school, running away from home, and being sent to juvenile detention.

Links to Risky Behavior

Drug and alcohol use have been linked to risky behavior in teenagers, specifically to engaging in unprotected sex and becoming involved in violent situations. Teens themselves admit that drugs and alcohol affect how they behave. In the 2010 CASA *National Survey on American Attitudes on Substance Abuse*, three out of four teens said that teens they know who drink alcohol or use illegal drugs are more likely to engage in sexual activity. Such activity often involves little or no protection against pregnancy or communicable diseases. Thomas R. Frieden, New York City's health commissioner, explains: "Heavy drinkers are more likely to have multiple partners—increasing their risk of HIV, other STDs, and unplanned pregnancy,"[12]

Teens who use alcohol or drugs also have an increased likelihood of engaging in violent behavior. In 2007, according to the US Office of National Drug Control Policy, young people who used an illicit drug were almost twice as likely as others to exhibit violent behavior. Additionally, in the same study one in four teens who abused illicit drugs reported attacking others with the intent to harm them.

Links to Crime

Drug and alcohol use have also been linked to juvenile delinquency. Studies indicate that the majority of teenagers who have been arrested or are currently residing in juvenile centers are either currently using or have used drugs and alcohol. In 2009, 53 percent of the teens arrested in San Diego County tested positive for at least one drug, and 94 percent reported having used drugs or alcohol at some point during their lifetime, according to the San Diego Association of Governments. Additionally, 88 percent of the teens arrested in San Diego County said they had used alcohol or marijuana by the age of 13.

Kristin is an example of how drug use can lead to criminal activity. Kristin started doing drugs by getting high on cough medicine when she was 15 years old. Kristin had been a straight A student, but her grades dropped after she started using cough medicine. She then moved on to nonmedical use of prescription drugs such as Oxycontin and morphine pills, which led to her becoming involved in criminal activity. She stole from a teacher and was arrested for theft, resulting in her confessing that she had a drug problem. "I finally had to come clean to them when I got arrested," writes Kristin. "I stole something from a teacher and she ended up finding out and called the police. When I told my parents I'd been doing drugs for years, they were dumbfounded."[13] At court the judge sent her to a rehabilitation center; since then Kristin has managed to stay away from drugs and hopes to build a drug-free future for herself.

> **Young people who used an illicit drug were almost twice as likely as others to exhibit violent behavior.**

Driving Under the Influence

One of the most dangerous behaviors associated with teenage drug or alcohol abuse is driving while high or intoxicated. Statistics show that driving under the influence is not uncommon among teenagers. According to the *2009 National Survey on Drug Use and Health*, an estimated 6.3 percent of 16- to 17-year-olds and 16.6 percent of 18- to 20-year-olds reported driving under the influence of alcohol in the past year.

Teenagers who drive while inebriated put their own and others' lives at risk. According to a 2007 Department of Transportation survey, motor vehicle crashes are the leading cause of death for 15- to 20-year-olds, and alcohol or drugs is the leading cause of these crashes. A person who drives in the United States with a blood alcohol concentration (BAC) level of 0.08 or higher is considered to be illegally driving because he or she is intoxicated. The National Highway Traffic Safety Administration found in 2006 that 25 percent of the young drivers aged 15 to 20 who were killed in crashes had BAC levels equal to or exceeding 0.08.

> One of the most dangerous behaviors associated with teenage drug or alcohol abuse is driving while high or intoxicated.

In 2006 Jessica Rasdall and her friend Laura Gorman spent hours drinking at a bar before Rasdall attempted to drive them home. Just a mile from Gorman's college dormitory, Rasdall lost control of the car and ran into a tree. Rasdall survived, but Gorman, her friend since kindergarten, died. "I would give anything to have been the one in the passenger seat that night. . . . Absolutely. No questions asked. . . . I would give anything to just bring her back,"[14] Rasdall says. Since the accident, Rasdall has served time in jail and started a website to warn other young people about making the same mistake.

Health Hazards

Drug and alcohol abuse can permanently damage the body. For example, long-term use of opiates like heroin can damage the veins, heart, and lungs. Ecstasy, even if taken only on a few occasions, may result in long-term brain damage. Methamphetamine can cause irreversible damage to the blood vessels in the brain and this damage can produce strokes. Long-term use of cocaine can result in heart disease, heart attacks, strokes, and seizures. Permanent brain damage can result from repeated use of inhalants, and taking more than the recommended dose of prescription drugs such as Oxycontin can lead to serious health problems including convulsions and coma.

Emergency room doctors and nurses throughout the United States see millions of people each year who are experiencing physical problems due to drug or alcohol use. SAMHSA's Drug Abuse Warning Network (DAWN) estimates that 2 million emergency room visits were due to the misuse and abuse of all drugs in 2008. Half of these visits involved illicit drugs such as cocaine and heroin; the other half involved nonmedical use of prescription or over-the-counter drugs.

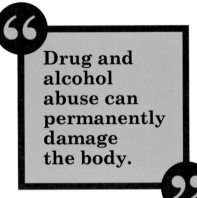

Drug and alcohol abuse can permanently damage the body.

Death is another hazard of drug and alcohol abuse. Years of alcohol abuse can damage the liver to the extent that it no longer functions. In these instances, only a liver transplant can prevent death, but livers are often not available for such operations. Excessive drinking has also been associated with increased risks of stroke and atrial fibrillation (abnormal heart rhythm), both of which can result in death. Drug overdoses also kill people. In 2007 the CDC logged more than 28,000 unintentional drug overdose deaths in the United States; more than half of these deaths involved opioid medications (such as oxycodone and methadone).

Damage to Teenage Brains

The teenage brain is particularly susceptible to damage from alcohol and drug abuse. Specifically, the prefrontal cortex, which is the part of the brain that allows people to understand situations and make sound decisions while keeping emotions and desires under control, is not fully matured in a teenager. Excessive use of alcohol or drugs can damage its development.

Recent studies show that heavy, ongoing use of alcohol by adolescents can have a long-term impact on brain functions such as learning and memory. When studying brain scans, scientists have seen that teens with alcohol-use disorders have significantly smaller volume in the hippocampus, the primary brain structure for memory, than do teens who do not abuse alcohol. "We're learning that heavy exposure to alcohol might adversely affect a part of the brain called the hippocampus, which is very critical to our ability to learn new information and to deeply encode it so that we can remember that information accurately later on,"[15] reports Susan Tapert, a neuroscientist and professor of psychiatry at the University of California at San Diego. Tapert worked on a study to see how binge drinking affected memory and other brain functions of teenagers.

Drugs Can Mask Other Problems

Teens who suffer from psychological disorders such as depression or bipolar disorder might turn to drugs and alcohol for relief. In doing this, however, they might actually mask underlying problems. This increases the risk of not getting proper treatment, which in turn means they are less likely to overcome their psychological disorders or their addiction. "Without proper treatment or recognition of their underlying mental problems, teens have a terrible time overcoming their dependence on their substances,"[16] states the Aspen Education Group, an organization dedicated to improving the lives of youth and their families.

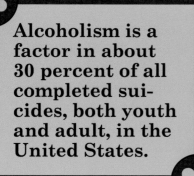

Alcoholism is a factor in about 30 percent of all completed suicides, both youth and adult, in the United States.

Young people who suffer from some form of depression are already at risk for suicide. Drug and alcohol abuse can increase that risk. For youths between the ages of 10 and 24, suicide is the third leading cause of death in the United States, resulting in approximately 4,400 young lives lost each year. According to the CDC, one of the risk factors of suicide is drug or alcohol abuse. The American Foundation for Suicide Prevention reports that alcoholism is a factor in about 30 percent of all completed suicides, both youth and adult, in the United States. "One of the risk factors associated with teen suicide is drug abuse," states the Teen Suicide Prevention website. "Drug abuse is one of those things that can really affect the chemical balance in the brain, intensifying feelings of depression and sadness."[17]

Life on the Streets

Teenagers who use drugs or alcohol risk ending up homeless and living on the streets. In some cases these teens have run away from home; in other cases they get kicked out. According to the US Department of Health and Human Services, 74 percent of homeless teenagers say that they used illicit drugs before leaving home, and about one-fifth report that drug use contributed to their leaving home.

Deshalle is an example of a young person who became homeless due to drugs and alcohol. She says that her addiction to both led her to becoming homeless while in her teens, living in and out of vacant buildings in downtown St. Louis, MO. Fortunately, Deshalle eventually heard about St. Patrick Center, a homeless service in Missouri, and through the center became sober and got a job. She now pays rent and is able to have her daughter live with her.

Deshalle was fortunate because, despite the fact that she was in a desperate situation, she was able to get help and start her life over. Unfortunately, this is not true for all teens who experience the dangers of substance abuse; many end up dealing with serious problems for the rest of their lives. All teens who use drugs or alcohol put themselves at risk for seriously damaging their lives.

What Are the Dangers of Teenage Drug Abuse?

66 The bottom line: Teenagers are more likely to experiment with drugs than people in other age groups. And, those experiments are more likely to produce addiction. 99

—Hazelden, "Changes in Brain Increase Risk of Teen Drug Addiction," 2010. www.hazelden.org.

Hazelden is a not-for-profit drug treatment facility with locations throughout the United States.

66 Drug abuse and addiction is the nation's deadliest disease, killing almost half a million people each year and destroying the lives of millions of families and friends. 99

—Joseph A. Califano Jr., "Statement by Joseph A. Califano, Jr. on the Government's National Survey on Drug Use and Health," National Center on Addiction and Substance Abuse at Columbia University, September 16, 2010. www.casacolumbia.org.

Califano is the chairman and founder of the National Center on Addiction and Substance Abuse at Columbia University.

* Editor's Note: While the definition of a primary source can be narrowly or broadly defined, for the purposes of Compact Research, a primary source consists of: 1) results of original research presented by an organization or researcher; 2) eyewitness accounts of events, personal experience, or work experience; 3) first-person editorials offering pundits' opinions; 4) government officials presenting political plans and/or policies; 5) representatives of organizations presenting testimony or policy.

> **Sexual assault . . . is far more likely to take place when alcohol abuse is involved. Alcohol reduces a person's inhibitions, making things such as sexual assault seem acceptable.**

> —Casa Palmera, "How Alcohol Abuse Can Lead to Sexual Assault and a Need for Alcohol Rehab," 2009. www.casapalmera.com.

Casa Palmera is a treatment center for people suffering from the disease of addiction and behavioral health disorders.

> **Since marijuana can affect judgment and decision making, using it can cause you to do things you might not do when you are thinking straight—such as risky sexual behavior, which can result in exposure to sexually transmitted diseases, like HIV, the virus that causes AIDS; or getting in a car with someone who's been drinking or is high on marijuana.**

> —"Western Nevada Regional Youth Center, "Marijuana, What Is It?" 2010. www.wnryc.org/teens/marijuana.html.

The Western Nevada Regional Youth Center is a an alcohol and drug treatment program.

> **Whether teens are experimenting with beer, wine, or other liquor, alcohol presents a serious—and potentially deadly—threat. Compared with non-drinking classmates, teens who drink are more likely to die in a car crash, get pregnant, flunk school, be sexually assaulted, become an alcoholic later in life, [or] take their own life through suicide.**

> —Mothers Against Drunk Driving (MADD), "Why Should You Care?" 2010. www.madd.org.

MADD is an organization with the mission to stop drunk driving and support the victims of this violent crime.

66 **When our son Ryan, then 18-years-old, was arrested for armed robbery while high on over-the-counter cough medicine, shocked doesn't even begin to describe how we all felt.** 99

—Christy Crandell, "Christy's Story," five moms, October 15, 2010. http://fivemoms.stopmedicineabuse.org.

Crandell is one of five moms whose teenagers' lives were negatively affected by cough medicine abuse. She and the other moms are using their teens' experiences to prevent others from abusing drugs.

66 **Since [ending up in the hospital for effects from ecstasy abuse] my life has been an uphill crawl, filled with doctors, therapists, meetings and a lot of soul searching. I have been placed on several medications such as anti-depressants, anti-psychotics and mood stabilizers, all to help me live with the chemical imbalance caused by my drug abuse.** 99

—Lynn Smith, "Agony from Ecstasy," Check Yourself, 2009. http://checkyourself.com.

Smith abused Ecstasy as a teenager until she landed in a hospital and then a mental institution.

66 **More than any other age group adolescents are at risk for substance addiction, and more than any other age group they risk permanent intellectual and emotional damage due to the effects of drugs.** 99

—Science and Management of Addictions (SAMA), "The Effects of Drugs and Alcohol on the Adolescent Mind," 2008. www.samafoundation.org.

SAMA is a privately funded nonprofit organization based in Seattle, WA. Its goal is to improve the management as well as the science of substance addiction.

What Are the Dangers of Teenage Drug Abuse?

- According to the New York Health Department, in 2009 New York teens who reported drinking any amount of alcohol in the past month were more than twice as likely as nondrinkers (**27 percent versus 11 percent**) to report having multiple sex partners.

- The New York Health Department reported in 2009 that condom use was less common (**63 percent**) among New York teens who reported using alcohol or drugs before sex than among those who were sober (**72 percent**).

- According to Mothers Against Drunk Driving, each year drinking among college students aged 18 to 24 contributes to an estimated **1,700 student deaths**, almost **600,000 injuries**, almost **700,000 assaults**, more than **90,000 sexual assaults**, and **474,000 incidents of engaging in unprotected sex**.

- The National Highway Traffic Safety Administration (NHTSA) reports that **1,510 persons** under age 21 were killed in alcohol-impaired driving crashes in 2008.

- In a study reported in a 2007 *Journal of Studies on Alcohol and Drugs*, **30 percent** of seniors in high school reported driving after drinking heavily or using drugs, or riding in a car whose driver had been drinking heavily or using drugs, at least once in the prior two weeks.

Youth Emergency Room Visits Rise Due to Nonmedical Use of Prescription Drugs

The Drug Abuse Warning Network shows that visits to emergency departments by 12- to 17-year-olds have increased each year from 2004 to 2008 due to misuse of prescription drugs. In 2008, an estimated 70,230 12- to 17-year-olds visited an emergency department due to nonmedical use of prescription drugs.

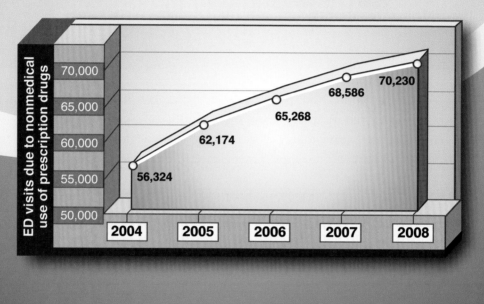

Source: Drug Abuse Warning Network, "National Estimates of Drug-Related Emergency Department Visits, 2004–2008," 2009. https://dawninfo.samhsa.gov.

- In 2008, according to the National Highway Traffic Safety Administration, of 15- to 20-year-old US drivers involved in fatal crashes, **31 percent** of the drivers who were killed had been drinking.

- SAMHSA's Drug Abuse Warning Network reports that the estimated number of emergency room visits for nonmedical use of prescription drugs increased **111 percent** from 2004 to 2008 (from 144,600 to 305,900 visits).

Drug Use Contributes to Teen Delinquency

The *2009 National Survey on Drug Use and Health* found that people aged 12 to 17 who had been involved in fights or other delinquent behaviors in the past year were more likely to have been using drugs in the past month than youth who were not doing drugs.

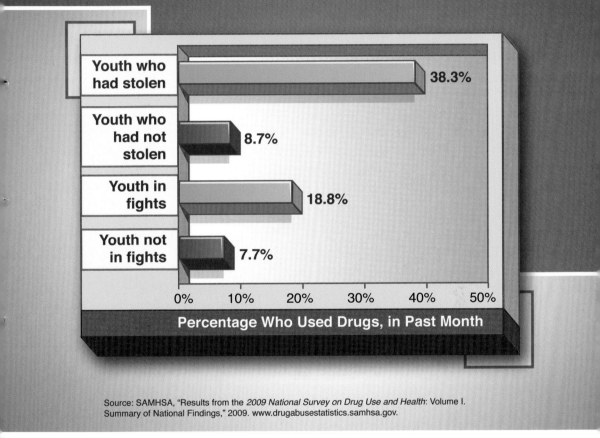

Youth who had stolen	38.3%
Youth who had not stolen	8.7%
Youth in fights	18.8%
Youth not in fights	7.7%

0%   10%   20%   30%   40%   50%

Percentage Who Used Drugs, in Past Month

Source: SAMHSA, "Results from the *2009 National Survey on Drug Use and Health*: Volume I. Summary of National Findings," 2009. www.drugabusestatistics.samhsa.gov.

- According to the National Institute on Drug Abuse, regular **abuse of inhalants** can permanently damage the brain and central nervous system due to the inhalants' poisonous fumes.

Drugs and Alcohol Lead to Risky Behavior

Drug and alcohol use among teenagers increases the likelihood of high-risk behavior. Sexual intercourse among teens is considered a high-risk behavior because it often leads to unintended pregnancies and sexually transmitted diseases. The Youth Risk Behavior Surveillance examined the links between teen sex and alcohol and drug use among ninth to twelfth graders in 42 states between 2008 and 2009. Out of 34.2 percent of students who identified themselves as sexually active, 21.6 percent said they drank alcohol or used drugs the last time they had sexual intercourse.

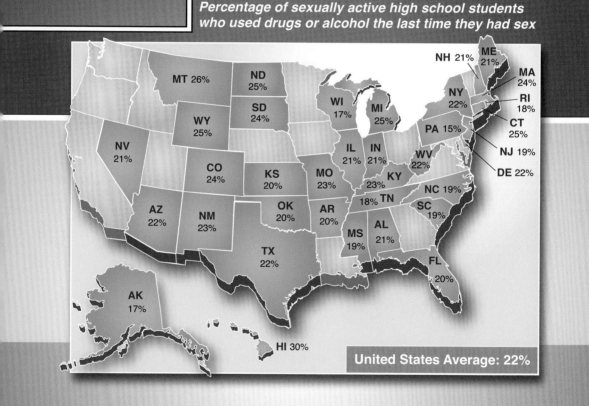

Percentage of sexually active high school students who used drugs or alcohol the last time they had sex

NH 21% ME 21%
MT 26%
ND 25%
NY 22%
MA 24%
RI 18%
WI 17%
MI 25%
PA 15%
CT 25%
SD 24%
WY 25%
NV 21%
IL 21% IN 21%
WV 22%
NJ 19%
DE 22%
CO 24%
KS 20%
MO 23%
KY 23%
NC 19%
TN 18%
SC 19%
AZ 22%
NM 23%
OK 20%
AR 20%
AL 21%
MS 19%
TX 22%
FL 20%
AK 17%
HI 30%

United States Average: 22%

Source: Centers for Disease Control and Prevention, "Youth Risk Behavior Surveillance—United States, 2009," 2010. www.cdc.gov.

- The American Foundation for Suicide Prevention reports that alcoholism is a factor in about **30 percent** of all completed suicides, both youth and adult, in the United States.

Young Drinkers Risk Alcohol Problems in Adulthood

The younger people are when they first use alcohol the more likely they will later abuse or become dependent on alcohol. According to the *2009 National Survey on Drug Use and Health*, adults who first tried alcohol at age 14 or younger were more likely to develop alcohol problems than people whose first use occurred at age 21 or older.

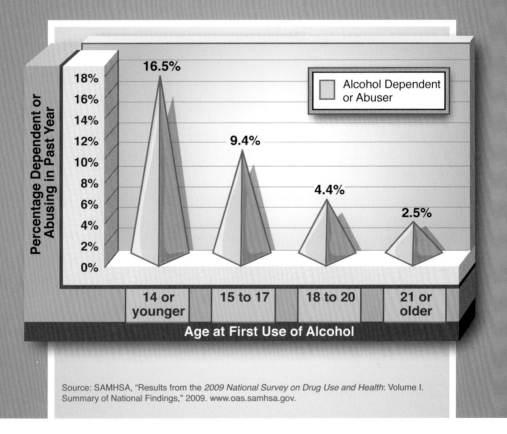

Source: SAMHSA, "Results from the *2009 National Survey on Drug Use and Health*: Volume I. Summary of National Findings," 2009. www.oas.samhsa.gov.

- According to studies by the Substance Abuse and Mental Health Services Administration, more than 1 in every 12 drug-related hospital emergency department visits by adolescents (**8.8 percent**) is due to a suicide attempt.

How Is Teenage Drug Abuse Treated?

A few days off the drugs, I felt it in my body. I started to realize that I was addicted, and I didn't want to end up a junkie. I knew I needed help and wanted to live a better life.

—Dave, a marijuana addict at age 18, telling about his first days at an on-site drug treatment center.

Recovery from a substance use disorder is more than abstinence. Recovery is about improving one's quality of life, being emotionally and physically healthy, succeeding in school or work, having healthy relationships, having a healthy social life, and living drug-free.

—Partnership for a Drug-Free America, *Treatment* (e-book).

Treatment While Young

The key to treating teenagers for substance abuse is to get them into treatment as soon as possible. Often teens believe they can beat the addiction on their own, but studies have shown that treatment increases the odds of achieving a stable recovery. A stable recovery means that the teen has remained sober for a significant amount of time without relapse. Relapse is a common occurrence among recovering drug abusers of all ages, but with continued treatment, a stable recovery is eventually possible. According to Michael Dennis, senior research psychologist at Chestnut Health Systems in Bloomington IL, "If treatment commences within the first decade of use this typically cuts in half the time it takes one to achieve recovery."[18]

Although there are different treatment options available to teens, none of these options is 100 percent successful and none will work without a lot of effort on the part of the teen. For any treatment to work, the teen must first admit that he or she has a problem.

Recognizing the Problem

Often teens do not realize that their substance use has spiraled into abuse. It typically takes a crisis or an intervention by friends and family to get them to understand they have a problem.

In Bill D.'s case, a crisis made him realize how drugs had taken over his life. Bill started using marijuana at age 15, and by the time he graduated from high school he was using Xanax, cocaine, Ecstasy, and crack. "I did not realize how truly grave my situation had become as I kept partying and feeding my drug addiction," writes Bill. "It was only after I suffered and had an accidental overdose and almost died that I was ready to face the truth and get the help I knew deep down I needed."[19] Bill decided to enter a treatment center and has since overcome his addiction.

For some teens, recognizing their problems requires intervention by their friends and families. During an intervention, the addict is brought into a room where his or her friends and family are waiting. Typically, an interventionist runs the meeting and has each loved one explain how the addict's substance abuse problem is negatively affecting his or her own and everyone else's lives. After listening to everybody, the addict decides whether to get treatment.

Difficulties with Treating Addicted Teens

Teenage addicts have different treatment needs than adult addicts. They are usually still in school and living at home and, in some cases, the home or neighborhood might not be conducive to staying away from drugs. Treatment programs designed for teenagers must take all of these needs into account in addition to addressing the usual needs of treating drug or alcohol addiction.

Finding such a program can be difficult, however. According to

SAMHSA's 2008 *National Survey of Substance Abuse Treatment Services*, only 30 percent of drug treatment programs surveyed had programs specifically for youth. And even those can be hard to get into, as many have long waiting lists.

Cost is also an issue. Many drug treatment programs, especially those that involve residential treatment, are very expensive. The typical teen addict stays in such a program for a few months, and often the cost can be as much as $7,000 per month. Families that do not have health insurance, or those that have insurance but no coverage for drug treatment, often cannot afford such programs.

12-Step Programs

Nearly all treatment programs incorporate the 12-step program, which is a set of principles for substance addicts to follow in order to recover from addiction. The steps include having the addicts admit that they are powerless to recover from alcohol or drug abuse on their own and that they need a "Higher Power" to attain and maintain sobriety. This program was originally created by Alcoholics Anonymous (AA) as a way to recover from alcoholism and is now used by the majority of substance abuse programs.

Alcoholics Anonymous and Narcotics Anonymous are among the most popular programs that center on the 12 steps. Both of these are self-help programs during which alcoholics or drug abusers attend facilitated meetings, discuss their abuse, listen to discussions on maintaining sobriety, work to follow the 12 steps, and are partnered with a mentor who has maintained sobriety. Most teens in AA and NA attend the meetings along with adults, but some communities have meetings specifically for teens.

> **Relapse is a common occurrence among recovering drug abusers of all ages.**

Some people think that the 12-step program is not a good fit for teenage drug and alcohol abusers because it requires participants to admit powerlessness against the addiction and rely on a "Higher Power" for help. Some believe that teaching teenagers that they have no control over their addiction could actually lead to continued drug or alcohol use.

Outpatient Treatment Programs

The most common way teen drug abusers get treatment is by attending an outpatient program specifically for youth. According to SAMHSA's *National Survey of Substance Abuse Treatment Services*, in 2008 more than 76,000 US teenagers were in outpatient treatment programs. Many parents choose these programs so that their teens can still live at home and attend school. This type of treatment also costs much less than a residential treatment center. Although costs vary, according to a SAMHSA study, outpatient treatment runs approximately $75 a day.

Nearly all treatment, including outpatient treatment, begins with detoxification. The teen must completely stop using drugs and allow his or her body to rid itself of all previous drugs. During withdrawal, emotional problems such as depression and sleeplessness may occur, while physical problems can include—in the case of alcohol—shakiness, nausea, convulsions, and hallucinations. Withdrawal from opiates, such as heroin or Oxycontin, can cause symptoms such as abdominal pain, agitation, nausea, diarrhea, and vomiting. Both outpatient and inpatient treatment centers oversee the detoxification process. Following detoxification, the work to discover the underlying cause of the teen's abuse and how to stop it occurs.

The High Focus Center in New Jersey offers a typical outpatient substance abuse treatment program for adolescents. Teens enrolled in its program attend two to four days each week after school, increasing or decreasing their visits on the basis of their progress during treatment. Throughout the program, teens attend meetings and therapy sessions that incorporate the 12-step program. Additionally, family therapy is included to help teens and their parents to better communicate, a key to a teen's recovery from substance abuse.

Residential Treatment Centers

The second most common way for teens to get treatment for substance abuse is by attending a residential treatment center where the teen remains 24 hours a day. In 2008 just under 10,000 teens were in residential treatment centers for substance abuse. These centers are a common choice for teens who relapse after attending an outpatient center, have a history of behavioral problems, live in an environment where close friends or family abuse substances, or are dealing with mental illness in addition to substance abuse. Teens in residential treatment centers are kept away from negative outside influences so they can concentrate on their recovery. At residential treatment centers, once detoxification is over, teens begin the process of changing their behaviors. A typical day at the Twelve Oaks Alcohol and Drug Treatment Center in Navarre, FL, begins with the teens exercising, then attending group therapy. Throughout the day they attend more therapy sessions and educational lectures about drugs and alcohol. Once a week, teens complete team-building initiatives and work on developing life skills such as time management and budgeting. At Twelve Oaks, teens also participate in pet therapy, where they work with dogs. This helps to foster compassion and responsibility in the teens, characteristics that have been found to help them recover. The center provides twice-weekly tutoring and coordinates with each patient's school to complete and turn in assignments.

> " Often teens do not realize that their substance use has spiraled into abuse. "

Cynthia S., a recovering substance abuser, attended a residential treatment center similar to Twelve Oaks. "While there I worked out my problems with my therapist. They taught me relapse prevention skills, to cope with things without using drugs and just how to live without the drugs,"[20] says Cynthia. Since then, Cynthia has attended Narcotics Anonymous meetings as part of her aftercare and continues to remain clean.

Medications to Treat Substance Abuse

In some cases, prescribed medications can help older teen drug users overcome their habits. These medications typically help addicts deal with withdrawal symptoms during detoxification or decrease their cravings for a substance, but teens must be 18 or 19 to get a prescription. Experts say that these medications need to be part of an overall treatment plan that includes behavioral therapy and addresses psychological dependence on substances.

An older teen alcoholic may be prescribed Antabuse to help him or her stop using alcohol. Antabuse interferes with the body's ability to process alcohol; drinking alcohol when taking Antabuse makes the drinker feel ill. It works by preventing the body from completely breaking down alcohol in the liver, which results in a buildup of toxic chemicals that lead to the ill feelings. Approximately 9 percent of alcoholics use Antabuse to help stop their drinking. However, a drawback of Antabuse is that it has caused severe and sometimes fatal liver problems in patients.

For teens who are addicted to opiates, Vivitrol, which was approved by the Food and Drug Administration in 2010 for people aged 18 and older, may be prescribed. Vivitrol is a nonnarcotic, nonaddictive medication that is administered in a once-a-month injection. Vivitrol decreases an addict's cravings by blocking receptors in the brain that cause the pleasurable effects of drug abuse. One of Vivitrol's drawbacks is that it is expensive, costing $1,100 a month and not yet covered by many health insurance plans.

When used, medication is usually only one part of treatment. Experts maintain that in all cases, with both teens and adults, a combination of therapy and medication is required to recover from substance abuse.

Maintaining Recovery

No matter the age of the user or the method of treatment, relapse is a common occurrence and often happens several times in a substance abuser's life. The National Institute on Drug Abuse reports that 40 to 60 percent of drug abusers and addicts who get treatment will relapse. According to Dennis, "While most of the adolescents who try using alcohol, marijuana or other drugs do not become addicted, one in four who start under the age of 15 end up developing abuse or dependence problems and do not stop until they have gone to treatment 3–4 times over several years."[21]

Treatment centers recommend that all patients, including teens, become involved with aftercare programs to help prevent a relapse. Narcotics Anonymous and Alcoholics Anonymous are among the best known aftercare programs and are attended by people of all ages. Other aftercare programs involve family or individual

> " The most common way teen drug abusers get treatment is by attending an outpatient program. "

> **Treatment centers recommend that all patients, including teens, become involved with aftercare programs to help prevent a relapse.**

counseling or attending meetings at a treatment center.

Aftercare has helped Krystan maintain sobriety. She became addicted to methamphetamine and alcohol when she was 13 years old. By age 16 she had attended inpatient and outpatient treatment centers but continued to relapse. At age 18 she again attended 30 days of inpatient treatment and then 30 days at a halfway house. She followed this up with regular attendance at facilitated self-help meetings and has remained sober since 1996. "Being clean and sober isn't always easy," Krystan writes. "What means the most to me is my family's support, going to meetings, talking and sharing my story, never forgetting where I came from, how I looked and how many people I really hurt."[22]

Krystan has since become an addiction and drug counselor to help other teens who suffered like she did. She maintains that recovery is possible, even though difficult. If teens who have battled substance abuse can maintain recovery, it is possible for them to get back on track and still live full lives.

How Is Teenage Drug Abuse Treated?

> **"A disease by its very nature is out of a person's control. This is simply not the case with substance abuse. Substance abusers make the choice to abuse alcohol and drugs. Choice is a behavior, not a disease."**

—The Saint Jude Retreats, "The Jude Thaddeus Program," 2009. www.soberforever.net.

The Saint Jude Retreats offer addiction treatment that is not based on the 12-step program but on the idea that addiction is the result of choices and within the addict's power to stop.

> **"Addiction is a terrible disease—and I emphasize disease. One of two things I ask patients is if they believe addiction is a disease or moral failing? If they say a moral failing, I say I respectfully disagree."**

—Howard Heit, "Q and A with Howard Heit, MD," MDNews, November 22, 2010. www.mdnews.com.

Heit is a physician with a specialty in addiction medicine.

Bracketed quotes indicate conflicting positions.

* Editor's Note: While the definition of a primary source can be narrowly or broadly defined, for the purposes of Compact Research, a primary source consists of: 1) results of original research presented by an organization or researcher; 2) eyewitness accounts of events, personal experience, or work experience; 3) first-person editorials offering pundits' opinions; 4) government officials presenting political plans and/or policies; 5) representatives of organizations presenting testimony or policy.

Primary Source Quotes

66 As the days went by, I got more involved with crystal meth and my new friends. One Tuesday afternoon, I got home about an hour late from school to find my family, Lisa and a lady there. They told me they cared about me. Not because I was just a sister, just a daughter, just a friend, but because I was Tory. They said they missed me. They called it an intervention. 99

—Tory, "My Name is Tory," Narconon, March 3, 2010. http://addiction.narcononrehab.com.

Tory became addicted to crystal meth in high school and after an intervention sought help and recovered from her addiction.

66 Nearly all addicted individuals believe at the outset that they can stop using drugs on their own, and most try to stop without treatment. Although some people are successful, many attempts result in failure to achieve long term abstinence. 99

—National Institute on Drug Abuse, "Principles of Drug Addiction Treatment: A Research Based Guide," April 2009. www.nida.nih.gov.

The National Institute on Drug Abuse is a part of the National Institutes of Health; its mission is to use the power of science to combat drug abuse and addiction.

66 Treatment for teens is scarce and often hard to find: although more than one million teens need drug treatment, only one in ten actually receive help. 99

—Mathea Falco, "Drug Treatment for Adolescents," HBO, 2010. www.hbo.com.

Falco is president of Drug Strategies, a nonprofit research institute in Washington, DC, that promotes more effective approaches to the nation's drug problem.

❝One advice I got from one member is to achieve a solid, well-balanced recovery. Maintaining mental, emotional, spiritual and physical balance in one's life is very important. If you do not pay attention to one of these areas, an addict may eventually relapse.❞

— I Addict, "How Not to Relapse into Your Addiction," Addict 4 Life, January 27, 2007. http://addict-4-life.blogspot.com.

An anonymous blogger who discusses his life as he works to maintain recovery from alcoholism.

❝The turning point for me in my sobriety was definitely changing the people, places and things and going to a halfway house straight from treatment and not taking any chances on going back home.❞

—David R, "Teen Story of Recovery: Marijuana Abuse," Inspirations, 2010. www.inspirationsyouth.com.

David R. is a recovering marijuana addict who attended Inspirations teen drug treatment center.

❝Sending a teen directly home to their old environment from drug treatment sometimes results in an endless cycle of relapse-treatment-relapse.❞

—Mark Greggston, "Breaking the Cycle of Teen Drug Abuse," One News Now, March 3, 2010. www.onenewsnow.com.

Greggston is an author, speaker, national radio host, and the founder of Heartlight, a residential counseling opportunity for struggling adolescents.

Facts and Illustrations

How Is Teenage Drug Abuse Treated?

- According to the 2008 Substance Abuse and Mental Health Services Administration (SAMHSA) *Summary Report: Caravan Survey for SAMHSA on Addictions and Recovery*, approximately **three-quarters** of the population believe that recovery from addiction to alcohol, prescription drugs, and marijuana is possible.

- The 2008 SAMHSA report found that **58 percent** of people in the United States believe that a person can fully recover from addiction to illicit drugs such as cocaine, heroin, or methamphetamine.

- According to the *2009 National Survey on Drug Use and Health*, 1.2 million youths aged 12 to 17 (**4.8 percent**) needed treatment for an alcohol problem.

- Of the 1.2 million youth with an alcohol problem, only **96,000** received treatment at a specialty facility.

- According to the *2009 National Survey on Drug Use and Health*, among youths aged 12 to 17, 1.1 million (**4.5 percent**) needed treatment for an illicit-drug problem.

- Of the **1.1 million** youth with an illicit-drug problem, only **115,000** received treatment at a specialty facility.

Treatment Options of Addicted Teens

Teenagers who have drug and alcohol problems have various treatment options. All require a significant time commitment. The cost of these programs varies, with residential programs easily running to thousands of dollars each month.

Treatment Setting	Description	Hours	What You Should Know
Outpatient	Client typically attends treatment at a specialty facility but lives at home. Many programs provide services in the evenings and on weekends so the individual can still attend school.	Teenagers typically attend treatment 6 hours per week or less.	You may be required to attend the program daily or weekly depending on the severity of substance abuse.
Intensive Outpatient	Client attends treatment during the day but lives at home. Treatment can last from 2 months to 1 year.	Teenagers typically attend treatment 6 hours per week or more.	This is for individuals who need multiple services, have any medical or psychological illnesses, or have not been successful in outpatient services.
Residential	These programs provide treatment services in a residential setting. Programs can last from 1 month to a year.	24 hours/day, 7 days/week	Typically, residents go through different phases as they progress through the program.
Inpatient	Treatment provided in specialty units of hospitals or medical clinics offering both detox and rehabilitation services.	24 hours/day, 7 days/week	Typically used for people with serious medical conditions or mental disorders.

Source: Partnership for a Drug-Free America, *Treatment Guide*. http://timetoact.drugfree.org.

Few Specialized Treatment Programs for Teens

Health professionals say that teenagers with substance abuse problems have special treatment needs. Treatment programs for teens must include components that address educational needs, family interaction, and issues involving peers. A national survey in 2008 found that few such programs for adolescents are available.

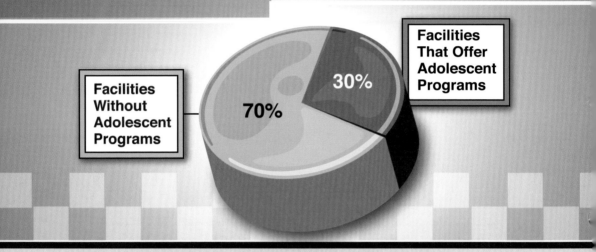

Facilities Without Adolescent Programs

70%

30%

Facilities That Offer Adolescent Programs

Total Facilities Surveyed: 13,688

Source: Substance Abuse and Mental Health Services Administration Office of Applied Studies, "National Survey of Substance Abuse Treatment Services (N-SSATS): 2008," 2008. wwwdasis.samhsa.gov.

- According to the *National Survey of Substance Abuse Treatment Services*, the average cost for inpatient drug rehabilitation programs is about **$7,000 per month**.

- Of those in need of but not getting substance abuse treatment, **33.7 percent** say it is because they either do not have health insurance or could not afford the cost of treatment.

- According to the National Institute on Drug Abuse, **40 to 60 percent** of drug abusers and addicts who get treatment will relapse.

Most Youth Attend Outpatient Treatment Programs

On March 31, 2008, there were 86,465 patients under age 18 in substance abuse treatment in the United States. The following chart shows a breakdown of those who attended inpatient treatment and those who attended outpatient. The majority of youth were in outpatient treatment programs, which allow teenagers to live at home and attend school while in treatment.

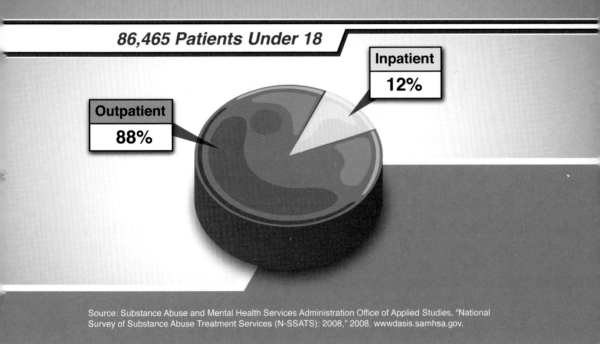

86,465 Patients Under 18

Inpatient
12%

Outpatient
88%

Source: Substance Abuse and Mental Health Services Administration Office of Applied Studies, "National Survey of Substance Abuse Treatment Services (N-SSATS): 2008," 2008. wwwdasis.samhsa.gov.

- According to its 2008 membership survey, **2.8 percent** of Alcoholics Anonymous members are under age 20.

- According to Drug Rehab Treatment, an educational website sponsored by CRC Health Group, about **3 percent** of the members of Narcotics Anonymous are under 20 years old.

- A 2008 study from Harvard Medical School and Massachusetts General Hospital found that for each AA/NA meeting that a youth in recovery attended, they gained **two days of sobriety**.

Can Teenage Drug Abuse Be Prevented?

"A child who gets through age 21 without smoking, using illegal drugs or abusing alcohol is virtually certain never to do so."

—Joseph A. Califano Jr., founder and chairman of the National Center on Addiction and Substance Abuse (CASA) at Columbia University.

"Structured activities and volunteering can help keep teens away from drugs, violence, and smoking while also boosting success in school."

—*Teen Drugs & Violence Report*, Office of National Drug Control Policy.

Having Conversations About Drugs

One of the best ways to prevent teenagers from abusing drugs and alcohol is for parents to talk to them honestly about the dangers of using these substances, say drug and alcohol addiction professionals. According to results of the annual Partnership for a Drug-Free America survey of young people in grades 6 through 12, those who report learning about the risks of drugs from their parents are nearly 50 percent less likely to use drugs than those who did not have these conversations with their parents. Yet in 2009 only 58.9 percent of youths aged 12 to 17 reported that they had talked at least once in the past year with at least one of their parents about the dangers of drug, tobacco, or alcohol use.

Tauny Ventura is one of the 58.9 percent of youths whose parents talked to them about drugs. Throughout her teen years various friends tried to persuade her to drink and do drugs, but she refused. "I'm grateful that both my parents were open and honest with me whenever I asked questions," writes Ventura. "They doled out lots of factual information regarding health issues and drugs, which I found really helpful. Despite my curious personality, their love, guidance, attention and support squashed any desires I might have had to drink or try drugs."[23]

Recognizing Risk Factors

Health professionals recommend that prevention programs focus on youth who are at high risk for becoming drug abusers. "The more risks a child is exposed to, the more likely the child will abuse drugs," states the National Institute on Drug Abuse.

> Some risk factors may be more powerful than others at certain stages in development, such as peer pressure during the teenage years; just as some protective factors, such as a strong parent-child bond, can have a greater impact on reducing risks during the early years. An important goal of prevention is to change the balance between risk and protective factors so that protective factors outweigh risk factors.[24]

Risk factors can be divided into personal, community, and family risk factors. Depression, ADHD, difficulty managing impulses, and a penchant for engaging in thrill-seeking behaviors are all considered personal risk factors. Community risk factors include attendance at a school where drugs and alcohol are prevalent or living in a neighborhood where drug and alcohol use is common. Family risk factors include households in which another family member abuses drugs or alcohol or where teenagers and parents have poor communication and possibly instances of verbal or physical abuse.

> "
> **Professionals recommend that prevention programs focus on youth who are at high risk for becoming drug abusers.**
> "

Transition periods in an adolescent's life also increase the risk for substance abuse. Advancing from elementary school to middle school, when young schoolchildren experience new academic and social situations, is one example. Moving to a new home and new school is another example of a major transition. A household in which parents are divorcing is a third example.

School Prevention Programs

Nationwide, several organizations conduct drug and alcohol prevention programs in schools and have helped reduce drug use among children and teens. According to the *2009 National Survey on Drug Use and Health*, in that year 74.9 percent of students aged 12 to 17 said that they had seen or heard drug or alcohol prevention messages at school. Studies show that these programs have helped teenagers resist peer pressure to try drugs and alcohol. In 2009 the use of illicit drugs was lower among students who reported having seen or heard prevention messages at school (9.2 percent) than those who had not heard or seen such messages (12.7 percent).

Not all drug prevention programs work equally well. One study found that programs that revolve around giving students information about drugs are less effective than programs that teach skills needed for resisting peer pressure, being more assertive, and making good decisions. D.A.R.E. (Drug Abuse Resistance Education) is one of the best-known and most successful school drug prevention programs in the United States. D.A.R.E. was founded in 1983 in Los Angeles and is now being implemented in 75 percent of US school districts and in more than 43 countries around the world. The D.A.R.E. curriculum is taught in schools by trained police officers and covers the dangers of drugs and crime. Statistics show that the D.A.R.E. program has benefited young people. A 2007 study found that of the 5,337 students surveyed who attended D.A.R.E. programs, 93 percent agreed that they learned new ways to make good and informed decisions about the use of alcohol, tobacco, and drugs, and 95 percent

> " As of 2008 an estimated 16.5 percent of school districts had adopted random drug testing programs. "

of the students felt attending the D.A.R.E. program helped them decide against using drugs in the future.

Another popular program is Project ALERT, a prevention program for middle school students. Project ALERT consists of 11 lessons typically taught once a week during the first year, plus 3 follow-up lessons that are delivered the following year. The lessons include role playing, videos, small group activities, and classroom discussions about the dangers of substance abuse and how to resist peer pressure. Teachers and others who use this program say they have seen good results. Cheryl Godwin, the Prevention Services coordinator of Ohio's Gallipolis City School District, writes about a student who attended Project ALERT classes:

> " **Monitoring social networking Internet sites can also help parents prevent teenagers from getting involved with drug and/ or alcohol use.** "

> This young man lives in a neighborhood where many people use drugs. The kids in the area view drug use as the norm. The student approached me and said his brother has been trying to get him to use marijuana. I asked him what he does and he says he tries some of the things he learned in Project ALERT like 'give an alternative.' He also said he sometimes has to 'stand up to pressure' and it has worked so far.[25]

Community Prevention Programs

Community substance abuse prevention programs aimed at teenagers use civic, religious, and law enforcement and other government organizations to teach antidrug messages. In 2009 approximately one in eight youths aged 12 to 17 (12.0 percent) reported that in the past year they had participated in drug, tobacco, or alcohol prevention programs outside of school.

One such program is the Border Binge-Drinking Reduction Program, which was established by the Substance Abuse and Mental Health Services Administration and is run by local police and other government agencies. This program's goal is to reduce young Americans' binge drinking across the US-Mexico border because such behavior often leads to car accidents and violence. Many young Americans cross the border to drink alcohol because it is legal for those 16 and older to drink in Mexico, and it is cheaper to drink there than in the United States. As a result, many youths under 21 cross the border and end up binge drinking.

> " The longer teenagers go without trying drugs and alcohol, the less likely they will eventually abuse or become addicted to drugs. "

The program works to prevent this binge drinking by conducting anonymous Breathalyzer tests to see what a person's blood alcohol level is upon returning to the United States. Sobriety checkpoints set up near the border also help catch young people who are driving drunk. In addition, bar owners in Mexico are being trained to detect fake IDs and turn away those using them.

Drug Testing

Random drug testing of students who are involved in extracurricular activities is being done in some school districts in hopes of preventing drug use. As of 2008 an estimated 16.5 percent of school districts in the United States had adopted random drug-testing programs. Drug tests are typically administered by medical professionals who randomly select students from a school activities' database on the day of testing. Students give a urine sample, and then the parents, students, and school officials are notified of the test results. If a student tests positive for a substance, he or she is not allowed to participate in the activity and is provided counseling. "The primary purpose of drug testing is not to punish students who use drugs but to prevent drug abuse and to help students already using become drug-free," states the National Institute on Drug Abuse. "The results of a positive drug test should be used to intervene with students who do not yet have drug problems, through counseling and follow-up testing."[26]

Although some critics believe that random drug testing is a violation of privacy, the US Supreme Court has upheld schools' rights to test students for drugs. Studies have shown that drug testing is an effective prevention method during the time students are involved in the activities that require random testing. According to an evaluation released in 2009 by the Institute of Education Sciences, 16 percent of students subject to drug testing reported recent use of substances covered by their district's testing compared with 22 percent of students in districts without such programs.

Web-Filtering Tools

Teenagers are able to find all kinds of information on the Internet. But the Internet has its downside, including information on drugs—where and how to get them and what to use. One way to keep teens from accessing this type of information is to use web-filtering tools. Some schools and some parents have installed these tools on computers used by teenagers.

Monitoring social networking Internet sites, such as Facebook and Twitter, can also help parents prevent teenagers from getting involved with drug and/or alcohol use. Sites like these provide tools that allow parents to monitor certain words (input by parents) used on their children's MySpace and Facebook pages. These tools allow parents to be alerted by e-mail with the context and location of those words if they appear on their teenager's profiles.

After-School Activities

Studies show that teen alcohol and drug use most often occurs between the hours of 3 and 6 p.m. Many teenagers are unsupervised during these hours immediately after school and prior to parents' arrival at home from work. Additionally, according to CASA's *National Survey of American Attitudes on Substance Abuse VIII*, teens are 50 percent more likely to drink, smoke, and use drugs out of boredom. If a teenager is not in school or involved in an after-school activity, he or she is more likely to be bored and in search of something to relieve the boredom.

For these reasons, teen participation in extracurricular activities has been found to be an important way to prevent teenage alcohol and drug abuse. These activities can be school related, such as sports or clubs, or community related, such as after-school programs, as long as they occupy teenagers and provide supervision.

Family Dinners

Studies show that teens from families that routinely eat dinner together are less likely to experiment with drugs and alcohol than teens from families that do not eat together. This subject was the focus of a 2009 study by the National Center on Addiction and Substance Abuse at Columbia University. That study found that teenagers who do not eat dinner with their families five to seven times per week are twice as likely to have used tobacco, nearly twice as likely to have used alcohol, and 1.5 times more likely to have used marijuana.

Increasing family time by eating together is just one of the many methods to help prevent teenagers from using drugs and alcohol. The longer teenagers go without trying drugs and alcohol, the less likely they will eventually abuse or become addicted to drugs. Ultimately, preventing a person from becoming a drug or alcohol abuser is easier than treating the problem once it develops.

Can Teenage Drug Abuse Be Prevented?

66 Drug-testing programs break down trust between students and administrators. They also carry the inherent danger of motivating some students to switch to drugs that will leave the system quickly, like alcohol, or drugs that [do] not show up in the tests, such as inhalants and herbal concoctions. 99

—Allie Brody, "Why I'm Standing Up Against Random Drug Testing at My High School," AlterNet, April 14, 2009. www.alternet.org.

Brody is a senior at Allentown High School in New Jersey and a founding member of Students Morally Against Random Testing.

66 Random drug testing can be a valuable means of finding out who is using drugs and putting a stop to the behavior. 99

—Jenny Tolley, "Public Schools Should Impose Mandatory Drug Testing on Students," Helium, 2010. www.helium.com.

Tolley is a writer with master's degrees in social work and public health.

Bracketed quotes indicate conflicting positions.

* Editor's Note: While the definition of a primary source can be narrowly or broadly defined, for the purposes of Compact Research, a primary source consists of: 1) results of original research presented by an organization or researcher; 2) eyewitness accounts of events, personal experience, or work experience; 3) first-person editorials offering pundits' opinions; 4) government officials presenting political plans and/or policies; 5) representatives of organizations presenting testimony or policy.

66 Most drug addicts started their drinking or experimentation with drugs at a very young age. Had teen
drug abuse prevention methods been instilled early in
their youth, they may have never turned to drugs or
alcohol in the first place. 99

—Drug Rehab, "Teen Drug Abuse Prevention Methods," 2010. www.drugrehab.com.

Drug Rehab is an organization that helps addicts find treatment programs and
promotes prevention efforts.

66 Research shows that the main reason that kids don't
use alcohol, tobacco, or drugs is because of their parents—because of their positive influence and because
they know it would disappoint them. That's why it
is so important that parents build a strong relation-
ship with their kids and talk to them about substance
abuse—the earlier the better! 99

—National Crime Prevention Council, "How Parents Can Prevent Drug Abuse," 2010. www.ncpc.org.

The National Crime Prevention Council's mission is to be the nation's leader in
helping keep people, their families, and their communities safe from crime.

66 The war on drugs will only be won by educating our
children about the dangers of drugs. 99

—Narconon Drug Prevention and Education, "The Narconon Drug Prevention Program," 2010.
www.drug-prevention.org.

The Narconon Drug Prevention and Education program has provided drug education programs to school children in Southern California for over 30 years.

66 Well-designed after-school activities can reduce the
risk that teens will use drugs. 99

—Office of National Drug Control Policy, "Keeping Our Children Safe, Healthy, and Drug-Free in the New School
Season," August 2010. www.theantidrug.com.

The Office of National Drug Control Policy works toward the reduction of illicit
drug use, drug-related crime and violence, and the manufacturing and trafficking
of drugs.

❝If I could wave a magic wand to make a dent in our nation's substance abuse problem, I would make sure that every child in America had dinner with his or her parents at least five times a week.❞

—Joseph A. Califano Jr., "Family Day," CASA, 2010. http://casafamilyday.org.

Califano is the founder and chairman of the National Center on Addiction and Substance Abuse (CASA) at Columbia University.

❝The wise parent would welcome independent monitoring of a teen's possible involvement with drugs. He or she will not be one of the foolish parents who insist, 'My child would never do that!' only to be proven tragically wrong at a later date.❞

—Carolyn Tytler, "Debate: Public Schools Should Impose Mandatory Drug Testing on Students," Helium, 2010. www.helium.com.

Tytler, a former elementary school teacher, is a parent and writer.

Facts and Illustrations

Can Teenage Drug Abuse Be Prevented?

- The 2009 Partnership Attitude Tracking Study (PATS), sponsored by MetLife Foundation, found that more than **one in five** parents felt unable to prevent their kids from trying drugs and alcohol.

- According to the *2009 National Survey on Drug Use and Health*, **58 percent** of youths aged 12 to 17 reported that in the past year they had talked at least once with at least one of their parents about the dangers of drug, tobacco, or alcohol use.

- The *2009 National Survey on Drug Use and Health* found that **90 percent** of youths reported that their parents would strongly disapprove of their trying marijuana or hashish once or twice.

- According to the *2009 National Survey on Drug Use and Health*, in that year almost four-fifths (**77 percent**) of youth reported having seen or heard drug or alcohol prevention messages from sources outside of school.

- A 2007 study found that of the 5,337 students surveyed who attended D.A.R.E. programs, **93 percent** agreed that they learned new ways to make good and informed decisions about the use of alcohol, tobacco, and drugs.

Fewer Youth Exposed to Prevention Messages

Not using drugs or alcohol is the only sure way to keep from developing a drug abuse problem. School and community prevention programs try to convey this message to teenagers. However, studies show that fewer youth are being exposed to substance abuse prevention messages both in and out of school.

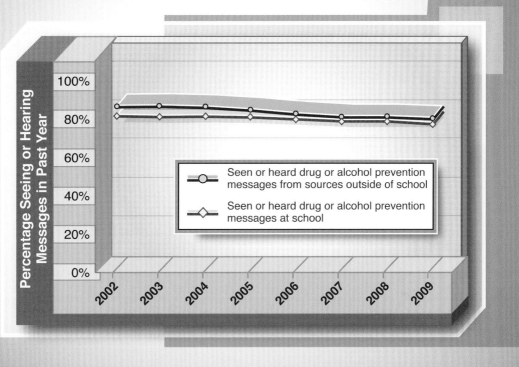

Source: U.S. Department of Health and Human Services, "*2009 National Survey on Drug Use and Health*," 2009. http://oas.samhsa.gov.

- The *2009 National Survey on Drug Use and Health* found that **75 percent** of school-enrolled youths reported that they had seen or heard prevention messages at school.

- The *National Survey of American Attitudes on Substance Abuse VIII* found that teens are **50 percent** more likely to drink, smoke, and use drugs out of boredom.

Close Family Ties Help Prevent Drug Use

The closer connection teenagers have with their parents, the less likely they will try alcohol, marijuana, or tobacco. CASA conducted a survey that found teens in families with weak family ties are more likely to have tried tobacco, alcohol, or marijuana than those with strong family ties.

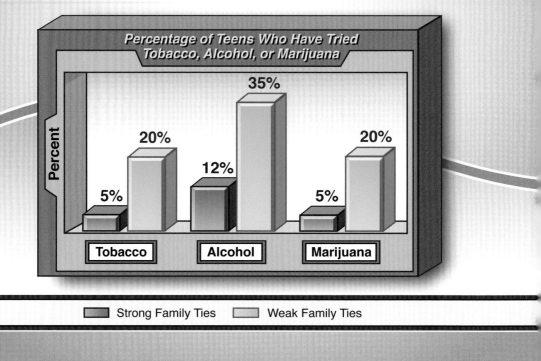

Percentage of Teens Who Have Tried Tobacco, Alcohol, or Marijuana

Tobacco — 5%, 20%
Alcohol — 12%, 35%
Marijuana — 5%, 20%

Percent

Strong Family Ties   Weak Family Ties

Source: The National Center on Addiction and Substance Abuse at Columbia University, *The Importance of Family Dinners VI*, September 2010. www.casacolumbia.org.

- A 2010 report by the National Center on Addiction and Substance Abuse (CASA) at Columbia University says that those teens who do not **eat dinner** with their families five to seven times per week are twice as likely to have used **tobacco** and nearly twice as likely to have used **alcohol** compared with teens who do eat dinner with their families five to seven times per week.

School Drug Testing Decreases Student Drug Use

The US Supreme Court has ruled that schools can require drug tests for students engaged in extracurricular activities. A US Department of Education study surveyed students at 36 high schools that do drug testing. The study showed that during the time the students were involved with their activities, those who could be randomly tested were less likely to use drugs than those who were in extracurricular activities but were not subject to testing.

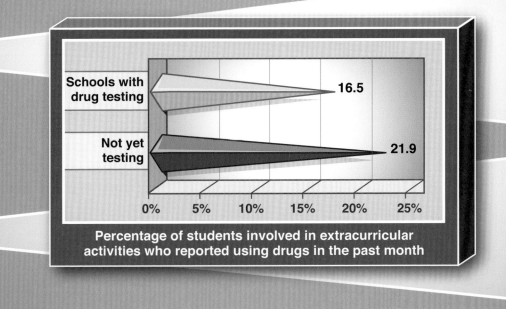

Schools with drug testing: 16.5

Not yet testing: 21.9

0% 5% 10% 15% 20% 25%

Percentage of students involved in extracurricular activities who reported using drugs in the past month

Source: Gret Toppo, "High School Drug Testing Shows No Long-Term Effect on Use," *USA Today*, July 14, 2010. www.usatoday.com.

- According to a 2007 Pew survey, **45 percent** of parents have monitoring software that records what their children do online.

- The 2007 Pew survey found that about **two-thirds** of parents of online teens report that they "check up" on their child after he or she has gone online.

Key People and Advocacy Groups

Alcoholics Anonymous (AA): A nonprofit organization with over 2 million members, AA was established in 1935 to help people recover from alcoholism by meeting regularly and following its 12-step method. Teen alcoholics can attend regular meetings or, in certain communities, youth meetings.

Joseph Califano: Califano is founder and chairman of the nonprofit National Center on Addiction and Substance Abuse (CASA) at Columbia University in New York City. Under Califano's leadership CASA conducts research and evaluates prevention and treatment programs involving all substances.

Drug Abuse Resistance Education (D.A.R.E.): D.A.R.E.'s mission is to give youth the skills they need to avoid involvement in drugs, gangs, and violence. Founded in 1983 in Los Angeles, this nonprofit program is now being implemented in 75 percent of US school districts and in more than 43 countries around the world.

Narcotics Anonymous: This nonprofit organization provides a 12-step recovery process and peer support network to drug addicts around the world. Approximately 3 percent of its members are under age 20.

National Institute on Drug Abuse: This organization is part of the National Institutes of Health. It leads national efforts to use science to fight drug abuse and addiction.

National Youth Anti-Drug Media Campaign: Congress created the National Youth Anti-Drug Media Campaign in 1998 with the mission of preventing and reducing youth drug use. Today, its advertising and online campaign encourage teens to live "above the influence" and reject the use of illicit drugs.

Barack Obama: As president of the United States, Obama oversees all US government policies, including those related to drugs and alcohol. In 2009 he declared September National Alcohol and Drug Addiction Recovery Month.

Stephen J. Pasierb: Pasierb is the chief executive officer and president of the Partnership for a Drug-Free America. He has led the organization since 2001 in the effort to help parents prevent drug and alcohol use by their children.

Students Against Destructive Decisions (SADD): SADD, a non-profit organization, was formed over 30 years ago to fight against student drunk driving. Today, its mission includes providing students with the best possible prevention tools to deal with underage drinking, other drug use, impaired driving, and other destructive decisions.

Betty Tai: Tai is the director of the Center for Clinical Trials Network of the National Institute on Drug Abuse. Tai leads projects that research behavioral, pharmacological, and integrated treatment interventions and determine the effectiveness of these treatments.

Nora D. Volkow: Volkow became the director of the National Institute on Drug Abuse (NIDA) at the National Institutes of Health in 2003. As leader of NIDA, she runs programs that support research on the health aspects of drug abuse and addiction.

Chronology

1920
The prohibition on the manufacture, sale, and consumption of alcohol goes into effect in the United States.

1935
Bob Smith and Bill Wilson found Alcoholics Anonymous.

1948
Wyeth Pharmaceuticals begins to sell Antabuse, the first medicine approved for the treatment of alcohol abuse and alcohol dependence by the US Food and Drug Administration.

1981
Students Against Driving Drunk is founded in Wayland, MA.

1920

1950

1980

1933
Prohibition ends in the United States.

1969
In a special message to Congress, President Richard Nixon identifies drug abuse as "a serious national threat."

1971
Nixon creates the Drug Enforcement Administration (DEA).

1937
Cannabis is made illegal in the United States with the passage of the federal Marihuana Tax Act.

1983
D.A.R.E. is founded as a community and school substance abuse and violence prevention program.

Chronology

1984
First Lady Nancy Reagan launches the "Just Say No" antidrug campaign as a way to fight youth drug abuse.

2010
President Barack Obama declares September 27, 2010, as Family Day, a day to join together by spending time with families as a way to help steer young people away from dangerous decisions, such as to abuse drugs and alcohol.

2009
The *2009 National Survey on Drug Use and Health* finds that an estimated 22.5 million persons in the United States are suffering from substance addiction or abuse; of these 1.8 million are 12 to 17 years old.

1993
The nicotine patch is developed and sold as an over-the-counter method to help people stop smoking.

1985

1995

2005

2010

1998
Congress creates the National Youth Anti-Drug Media Campaign to prevent and reduce youth drug use.

2001
The Substance Abuse and Mental Health Services Administration (SAMHSA) estimates that over 11 million people have taken prescription drugs for nonmedical uses at least once in their lifetime.

1989
President George H.W. Bush creates the Office of National Drug Control Policy (ONDCP) and appoints William Bennett as his first "drug czar."

2008
SAMHSA's *National Survey of Substance Abuse Treatment Services* finds that more than 76,000 youth are in outpatient substance abuse treatment programs.

Related Organizations

American Academy of Child & Adolescent Psychiatry (AACAP)

3615 Wisconsin Ave. NW
Washington, DC 20016-3007
phone: (202) 966-7300 • fax: (202) 966-2891
e-mail: communications@aacap.org • website: http://aacap.org

The AACAP is a nonprofit professional medical association dedicated to treating and improving the quality of life for children and adolescents affected by mental, behavioral, or developmental disorders. One of its goals is to educate people about the consequences of teen substance abuse.

American Society of Addiction Medicine

4601 N. Park Ave., Upper Arcade #101
Chevy Chase, MD 20815
phone: (301) 656-3920 • fax: (301) 656-3815
e-mail: email@asam.org • website: www.asam.org

This organization's mission is to improve the quality of addiction treatment and provide physicians the latest information about addiction medicine for both adults and youth. Additionally, this group is involved in substance abuse prevention methods.

The Courage to Speak Foundation

PO Box 1527
Norwalk, CT 06852
phone: (877) 431-3295
website: www.couragetospeak.org

This organization was founded in 1996 after the founders, Ginger and Larry Katz, lost their son to a drug overdose. Their mission is to incorporate drug and alcohol prevention programs into school health curricula, first at the middle school level, then in high school and elementary schools.

CRC Health Group

20400 Stevens Creek Blvd., 6th Floor
Cupertino, CA 95014
phone: (877) 637-6237 • fax: (408) 367-0030
website: www.crchealth.com

CRC Health Group is a provider of treatment and educational programs for adults and youth who are struggling with many issues, including substance addiction. This organization sponsors ASK, a website that provides information about prevention and treatment of youth substance abuse.

Join Together

580 Harrison Ave., 3rd Floor
Boston, MA 02118
phone: (617) 437-1500 • fax: (617) 437-9394
e-mail: editor@jointogether.org • website: www.jointogether.org

Formed in 1991, Join Together works to support community-based efforts to advance effective alcohol and drug policy, prevention, and treatment with specific programs for youth. This organization leads initiatives to help communities respond to the damage caused by alcohol and drug abuse among adults and youth.

National Center on Addiction and Substance Abuse (CASA) at Columbia University

633 Third Ave., 19th Floor
New York, NY 10017-6706
phone: (212) 841-5200
website: www.casacolumbia.org

Former secretary of health, education, and welfare Joseph A. Califano Jr. founded the National Center on Addiction and Substance Abuse (CASA) at Columbia University in 1992. This nonprofit organization conducts surveys and provides information about youth drug use and prevention methods.

NIDA for Teens

6001 Executive Blvd., Room 5213
Bethesda, MD 20892-9561
phone: (301) 443-1124
e-mail: information@nida.nih.gov • website: http://teens.drugabuse.gov

The National Institute on Drug Abuse for Teens educates teens and their parents about the science behind drug abuse. Its website provides information about the dangers of substance abuse, how teen brains are affected by substances, and personal stories of teen drug abuse.

Office of National Drug Control Policy

PO Box 6000
Rockville, MD 20849-6000
phone: (800) 666–3332 • fax: (301) 519–5212
website: www.whitehousedrugpolicy.gov

Established in 1988, the White House Office of National Drug Control Policy is part of the executive office of the president. Its main goal is to establish policies, priorities, and objectives for the nation's drug control program specifically in the areas of illicit drug use, manufacturing and trafficking, drug-related crime and violence, and drug-related health consequences.

Partnership for a Drug-Free America

405 Lexington Ave., Suite 1601
New York, NY 10174
phone: (212) 922-1560 • fax: (212) 922-1570
website: www.drugfree.org

The Partnership for a Drug-Free America is a nonprofit organization that engages parents, scientists, and communications professionals to help families raise drug-free children. The partnership provides parents with information and training tools that they can use to help prevent their children from using drugs and alcohol.

Substance Abuse and Mental Health Services Administration

PO Box 2345
Rockville, MD 20847-2345
phone: (877) 726-4727) • fax: (240) 221-4292
e-mail: shin@samhsa.hhs.gov • website: www.samhsa.gov

This agency works to help people who are in need of recovery from or at risk for mental or substance use disorders. SAMSHA publishes up-to-date information about drug addiction and treatment with specifics about youth drug and alcohol use. It also provides grants for research on substance abuse and mental disorders among adults and youth.

For Further Research

Books

Jarold Imes, *Never Too Much—the Remix*. Winston-Salem, NC: Abednego's Free, 2008.

Ann Kramer, *Drugs (FAQ)*. London: Franklin Watts, 2010.

David Sheff, *Beautiful Boy*. New York: Houghton Mifflin, 2008.

Jennifer Storm, *Blackout Girl: Growing Up and Drying Out in America*. Center City, MN: Hazelden, 2008.

Virginia Vitzthum, Laura Longhine, and Keith Hefner, *The High That Couldn't Last: Teens and Drugs, from Experimentation to Addiction*. New York: Youth Communication, 2010.

Hannah Westberg, *Hannah: My True Story of Drugs, Cutting, and Mental Illness*. Deerfield Beach, FL: HCI Teens, 2010.

Periodicals

Jane Anderson, "Youth Drinking Yields Emergencies," *Pediatric News*, September 2010.

John Cloud, "Can One Drug Addiction Cure Another?" *Time*, March 8, 2009.

John Cloud, "This Ain't No Wine Cooler," *Time*, July 17, 2008.

Rochelle Craig, "Teenage Addicts Are Not Born Bad, They Have a Disease," *Daily Mail* (London), October 5, 2010.

Economist, "One Success in the Drug Wars," May 1, 2008.

Neil Johnson, "Alcohol, Drugs Slow Teen Development," *Janesville* (WI) *Gazette*, March 17, 2010.

Leicester Mercury (UK), "The Problem for Youngsters Is Boredom," September 22, 2010.

New York Times Upfront, "The Truth About "Rehab" & Drug Addiction: The Reality Is Far from Glamorous," April 6, 2009.

Garrett O'Connor, "Doctor's Role in the Prescription Drug Crisis," *Addiction Professional*, July/August 2010.

PR Newswire, "Upcoming FDA Hearing on Abuse of Cough and Cold Medications Misses the Mark," September 14, 2010.

Carol Reiter, "Teens' Abuse of Prescription Pills on the Rise," *Buffalo (NY) News*, April 27, 2010.

Science World, "Straight Talk on Prescription Drugs: A Teen Reporter Interviews the Director of the Nation's Leading Research Agency on Drug Abuse and Addiction," October 18, 2010.

Maia Szalavitz, "Does Teen Drug Rehab Cure Addiction or Create It?" *Time*, July 10, 2010.

Topeka (KS) Capital-Journal, "Bad Policy," October 22, 2010.

Nora Volkow, "The Truth About "Rehab" and Drug Addiction," *Science World*, April 6, 2009.

Internet Sources

Drug Addiction Treatment, "Teen Heroin Addiction Growing Rapidly in Seattle," November 4, 2010. www.drugaddictiontreatment.com/addiction-in-the-news/addiction-news/teen-heroin-addiction-growing-rapidly-in-seattle.

Mathea Falco, "Drug Treatment for Adolescents," HBO, 2010. www.hbo.com/addiction/treatment/35_treatment_for_adolescents.html.

Bill Hendrick, "Family Dinners Reduce Teen Drug Use," WebMd, September 22, 2010. www.webmd.com/parenting/news/20100922/family-dinners-reduce-teen-drug-use.

National Institute on Drug Abuse, *Monitoring the Future Survey: Overview of 2008 Results*, April 2, 2009. www.nida.nih.gov/newsroom/08/MTF08Overview.html.

Office of National Drug Control Policy, "Youth Drug Use Down Since 2002, According to New National Survey," September 10, 2009.

Source Notes

Overview

1. Quoted in Steven Reinberg, "At U.S. Colleges, Binge Drinking Is on the Rise," Health, *U.S. News & World Report*, June 15, 2009. http://health.usnews.com.
2. Megan Hakeman, "Addicted to Inhalants," Check Yourself, 2009. http://checkyourself.com.
3. Quoted in Donna Leinwand, "Prescription Drugs Find Place in Teen Culture," *USA Today*, June 13, 2006. www.usatoday.com.
4. Quoted in Matt Elofson, "Two Meth Addicts Tell Life Recovery Story," *Dothan (AL) Eagle*, August 15, 2010. www2.dothaneagle.com.
5. Quoted in Richard Knox, "The Teen Brain: It's Just Not Grown Up Yet," NPR, March 1, 2010. www.npr.org.
6. Quoted in Kelley Weiss, "Binge Drinking on the Rise for Younger Teens," Capital Public Radio, November 11, 2008. www.capradio.org.

How Serious Is Teenage Drug Abuse?

7. American Academy of Child and Adolescent Psychiatry, "Teens: Alcohol and Other Drugs," May 2008. http://aacap.org.
8. Nicole Hansen, "Real Drugs, False Friends," Check Yourself, 2009. http://checkyourself.com.
9. Quoted in Marketwire, "CASA 2007 Teen Survey Reveals America's Schools Infested with Drugs," August 16, 2007. www.marketwire.com.
10. Casa Palmera, "Drug Abuse and Depression in Teens," 2009. www.casapalmera.com.
11. Quoted in National Center on Substance Abuse and Addiction at Columbia University, "You've Got Drugs," July 9, 2008. www.casacolumbia.org.

What Are the Dangers of Teenage Drug Abuse?

12. Quoted in New York City Department of Health and Mental Hygiene, "Health Department Report Links Heavy Drinking to Increased Risk of HIV and Other STDs," January 5, 2009. www.nyc.gov.
13. Kristin, "Sippin' Cough Syrup," WebMD, 2009. www.webmd.com.
14. Quoted in Alan Goldberg, "Drunk Driving Crash Shattered Teen's Life," ABC News, June 2, 2009. http://abcnews.go.com.
15. Quoted in NPR, "Study: Teen Drinking Can Have Lifelong Effects," February 1, 2010. www.npr.org.
16. Aspen Education Group, "Dual Diagnosis Teens: When Drinking and Drugging Is Really Something Else," 2009. www.aspeneducation.com.
17. Teen Suicide Prevention, "Teen Drug Abuse," 2005. www.teensuicide.us.

How Is Teenage Drug Abuse Treated?

18. Michael Dennis, "Inpatient or Outpatient? How to Find and Evaluate Adolescent Treatment," HBO, 2010. http://edition.cnn.com.
19. Bill D., "Testimonial," Transformations Drug and Treatment Center, 2008. http://transformationstreatment.com.
20. Cynthia S., "Teen Story of Recovery—Prescription Drug Abuse," Inspirations, 2010. www.inspirationsyouth.com.
21. Dennis, "Inpatient or Outpatient?"

22. Krystan, "I Was Tired of Nobody Trusting Me," Check Yourself, 2009. http://checkyourself.com.

Can Teenage Drug Abuse Be Prevented?

23. Tauny Ventura, "My Xtreme Life," Check Yourself, 2009. http://check yourself.com.
24. National Institute on Drug Abuse, "Preventing Drug Abuse Among Children and Adolescents." www.drug abuse.gov.
25. Quoted in Project ALERT, "Project ALERT Works," 2010. www.projec talert.com.
26. National Institute on Drug Abuse, "Frequently Asked Questions About Drug Testing in Schools," September 2007. http://drugabuse.gov.

List of Illustrations

How Serious Is Teenage Drug Abuse?

What Are the Dangers of Teenage Drug Abuse?

How Is Teenage Drug Abuse Treated?

Can Teenage Drug Abuse Be Prevented?

List of Illustrations

Index

Note: Boldface page numbers indicate illustrations.

About the Author

Leanne K. Currie-McGhee lives in Norfolk, VA, with her husband, Keith, and two daughters, Hope and Grace. She has been writing educational books for several years.